ENGLISH RECUSANT LITERATURE
1558–1640

Selected and Edited by
D. M. ROGERS

Volume 339

FRANCISCO ARIAS
A Treatise of Benignity
1630

MATTHEW WILSON
A Direction to be Observed by N. N.
1636

FRANCISCO ARIAS

A Treatise of Benignity

1630

The Scolar Press

1977

ISBN o 85967 375 8

Published and printed in Great Britain by
The Scolar Press Limited, 59-61 East Parade,
Ilkley, Yorkshire and
39 Great Russell Street,
London WC1

NOTE

The following works are reproduced (original size) with permission:

1) Francisco Arias, *A treatise of benignity*, 1630, from a copy in the library of St. Edmund's College, Ware, by permission of the President. This copy lacks the third and fourth leaves, which are reproduced in the facsimile from a copy in the library of the Brompton Oratory, by permission of the Provost and Fathers.

Reference: Allison and Rogers 40; not in STC.

2) Matthew Wilson, *A direction to be observed by N. N.*, 1636, from a copy in Cambridge University Library, by permission of the Syndics.

References: Allison and Rogers 895; STC 25777.

A
TREATISE
OF
BENIGNITY.

WRITTEN BY FATHER
FRANCIS ARIAS, OF THE
Society of IESVS, in his second
parte of the Imitation of Christ
our Lord.

Translated into English.

Estote inuicem Benigni, misericor-
des, donantes inuicem, sicut &
Deus in Christo donauit vobis.

Be benigne to one an other, mercifull, pardoning one an other, as
God in Christ hath pardoned you.

With permission of Superiours
Anno 1630,

TO THE READER.

GOOD Reader,
The tráſlatour of
the treatice of *Pa-*
tience lately printed, had
alſo rendred this of *Benig-*
nity out of rhe ſame Autour: but it came not in
time to be diſpatched with
it; & therefore goeth here
a parte by it ſelfe. It will
ſerue no leſſe then that o-

    ★ ₂   ther

ther of *Patience* to inamour vs with *Chriſt* our Lord, if we will conſider the vnſpeakable ſweetneſſe of his charity, whileſt he made the world happy by conuerſing in it. The particulars whereof thou ſhalt finde, Good Reader, admirably expreſſed in this treatice by this holy Autour; which is therefore recommended vnto thee.

A TABLE

A TABLE OF THE
CHAPTERS.

THE I. CHAPTER.

A Table

con-

A Table

The

A TREA-

A TREATISE OF THE VERTVE OF BENIGNITY,

wherein the nature thereof is declared, together with the operations and exercifes of the fame, and the examples thereof, which Chrift our Lord gaue vs. Tráflated out F. Frácis Arias of the Society of Iefus, in his 2. part of the imitation of Chrift our Lord.

THE I. CHAPTER.

In what the vertue of Benignity confifteth; and how Chrift our Lord difcouered it, in the Myfteries of his Incarnation, Natiuity, and Apparitō to the Shepheards, and to the vocation of the Gentiles in the perfon of the Magi.

T He vertue of Benignity confifteth in that a man defire,

A and

and difpofe himfelfe to doe good
to his neighbour, whofoeuer he
be; and in that he do it from the
hearte; yea and with a fweet and
tender kinde of will; and in that
he put this will in execution by
doing good indeed to his neighbour; and in that he do it abun-
dantly, if it be in his power; and
laftly in that it be with a kinde of
contentment, and ioy. It doth
alfo confift in that a man treate
& conuerfe with his neighbours
after a fweet and gentle manner,
condefcending to them, and giuing them guft in any thing,
which is lawfull, and agreable to
the feruice of God; and behoulding them with a clear, and dif-
charged countenance, and fpeaking to them in fweet and gentle
words.

There are men, who in very
truth haue the effentiall part of
                              the

the vertue of Charity with their
neighbours, both friends, & enemies ; both wishing them good,
and performing it to them: but
yet they fall short, in remedying
their necessities according to
their ability ; and they are au-
stere and sharpe in their conuersation, and dry and vntoward in
performing the very good, which
they doe.

The vertue of *Benignity*, doth
cure and heale a man of all these
defects ; making him who is the
owner of it, to loue his neighbour hartily, and sweetly; and to
doe him good liberally & cheerfully; and to conuerse with him
affably and gently, auoyding
(for as much as the lawe, & good
pleasure of God will permit) all
that which may giue him any dif-
gust, or paine. And so, *Benignity*
falls out to be, the act and exer-

A 2   cise

cife of *Charity*, with that perfection, which wee haue declared;
and interiourly it embraceth the
act of beneuolence and loue;and
exteriourly the exercife of bene-
ficence, liberality, affability,and
of all fweetnes in conuerfation.
It is alfo one of *the fruites of the*
Holy Ghoft; For an act of vertue,
in regard that it proceedeth frõ
thence, and giueth guft to him
who performeth it, is called a
fruite; and therefore *Benignity*
being an act of *Charity*, and cau-
fing delight in him,by whom it is
poffeffed, is accounted *amongft*
the fruits of the Holy Ghoft. All this
is confeffed by the Saints, when
they fpeake of *Benignity*. Saint *Ifi-*
dorus faith; That man is faid to be
Benigne, who doth good with a
good will, and vfeth fweetnes in
his wordes. A d Saint *Anfelmus*,
declaring what *Benignity* is, faith
                              thus,

thus; *Benignity* is a good affection
of the will, & a serenity of heart;
in vertue whereof a man doth,
for Gods sake giue all he can, after a gratious and cheerfull manner; and difcourfeth and conuer-
feth gently, and fweetly with his
neighbours. And Saint *Thomas,*
explicating the nature of *Benig-*
nity, faith, that it is the very fweetnes & tendernes of *Charity,* which
fpreads, & communicates it felf
exteriourly; & that as natural fier
doth melt mettel, & make it flow;
fo the fier of loue, which is *Benig-*
nity, maketh a mā fcatter what he
hath towards the fuccour of the
neceffities of his neighbours.

This is that, which the Saints
fay of *Benignity,* and the fumme of
it all is this: that it is the tendernes of *Charity,* which doth not
only communicate a mans exteriour goods to his neighbour, but

A 3　　　　toge-

together with them , it communicates his owne very bowells;
which is , to difcouer both by
wordes, and workes , the dearnes
& fweetnes of *Charity*. The Apoftle declareth this , by faying ,
Charity is Benigne . Which fignifieth, that it makes the man who
poffeffeth it , not to be ftraight
handed, but apt to communicate
his goods; and not to be harfh or
bitter; but that he communicate
euen his very hart by conuerfing
with all men after an affable and
fweet manner. And to giue vs to
vnderftand this truth , the holy
Scripture, doth by one & the felfe
fame Hebrew, and Greeke word,
which fignifieth *Benignity* in doing
good, fignify alfo a foftnes, and
fweetnes in the manner of fhewing mercy. And fo, whereas *Dauid*
faith; *Our Lord is sweet towards all,*
another letter faith , *Our Lord is*
benigne

benigne towards all. And whereas he
faith, *That mā is gentle, & sweet, who
sheweth mercy*; another tranſlation
faith; *The man who sheweth mercy, is
Benigne.* And therfore S. *Baſil,* when
he would explicat what it was, for
a man to be *Benigne,* faith; that it
is he, who doth liberally enlarge
himſelfe to doe good to all ſuch
as are in neceſſity. And he confir-
meth it by that Pſalme which
faith, *Our Lord is benigne towards
all*; and by that other, which alſo
faith, *That a man is Benigne, who
sheweth mercy,* and imparteth his
goods to ſuch as are in neceſſity.

In this *Benignity* did *Chriſt* our
Lord inſtruct vs, and perſwade vs
to it, by many examples, & Myſteries of his holy life which wee
wil édeauour to declare. The firſt
and principall Myſtery, wherein
he diſcouered his *Benignity,* was
that of his *Incarnation.* In that, the

A 4   moſt

moſt high ſonne of God was pleaſed to become a naturall man, & to appeare viſibly in the world in mortall fleſh, obnoxious to the miſeries and penalties of other men; and in that he did all this, to doe good to man; and to draw him to his loue, and ſo to ſaue him; not onely did he diſcouer an immenſe loue towards vs, but a loue which was alſo moſt ſweet and dear. And not onely did he communicate his bleſſings to vs, but he alſo did it with ſupreme liberality, and guſt, and ioy of his owne ſacred heart. And together with his bleſſings, he communicated to vs, his very ſelfe; namly his body, his blood, his bleſſed ſoule, and his diuinity; and all that which he hath, yea and euen all that which he is, he communicated to vs, by many admirable & myſterious waies. This did the

the Apoſtle ſignify by ſaying;
Whē in the time of grace, the *Be-*
nignity & imméſe loue of our God
and Sauiour to man, did manifeſt
it ſelfe to the world, he ſaued and
freed vs from our ſinnes, not by
the title of Iuſtice, and the merit
of our workes, (which were not of
any valew without *Chriſt* our
Lord, for the arriuing to that
end;) but through his owne great
mercy, and moſt gratious boūty,
and by meanes of that ſacred La-
uatory, which is holy Baptiſme,
whereby wee are engendred a ſecond time to be the ſonnes of
God, and renewed by a ſpirituall
generation, & renouation, which
is wrought by the holy Ghoſt ;
which Holy Ghoſt, the eternall
Father hath by meanes of his
gifts and graces infuſed and cōmunicated to vs in great abun-
dāce, through the merits of *Chriſt*

A 5   our

our Lord , to the end that being
iuſtified through the grace of the
ſame Lord , wee might from this
inſtant become heires of eternall
life, which now wee hould by certaine hope , and which hereafter
wee ſhall haue in actuall poſſeſ-
ſion . This is deliuered by Saint
Paule . And Saint *Bernard* , vpon
theſe words, declaring that *Benignity* of God which was diſcouered
in this Myſtery diſcourſeth thus.
Before the humanity of *Chriſt* our
Lord appeared in the word the
Benignity of God was hidden from
vs. There was already in God this
Benignity, & mercy, which in him
is eternall ; but ſo great *Benignity*
as this , was not knowen before,
nor was there any meanes how to
to know it. And although it were
promiſed by the Prophets , yet
men vnderſtood it not , and felt
it not, and many did not ſo much

a

as beleeue it. But when that time
arriued, which had been ordained by the diuine wifedome, Almighty God came in mortall
flefh, and being vefted with his
facred *Humanity*, and appearing
to the eyes of our flefh & blood,
his *Benignity* came to be made
knowne; for by no meanes could
he more haue manifefted his *Benignity*, then by taking our flefh;
and by no meanes could he more
haue declared his mercy, then by
vndertaking our mifery. Let mā
confider, and vnderftand from
hence, how great care God hath
of him; and how much he eftee-
meth him; and for how mighty
an end he made him; fince he did,
and fuffered fo great thinges for
him. And thus, by his *Humanity*
wee may know his *Benignity*; for
how much the leffe he became by
his *Humanity*, fo much the grea-

A 6   ter,

ter doth he shew himselfe to be in bounty; and by how much the more he abased himselfe for vs, so much the more amiable doth he shew himselfto vs. This is said by Saint *Bernard* ; and so it is a most clear truth , that nothing hath made so great discouery to vs of the bounty, and *Benignity* of God, nor hath moued & obliged vs so to loue and praise him , as for that he hath taken our *Humanity*. And therfore as Dauid saith, *giue praise to God, because he is benigne and good; and sing praises to his name, because he is sweet.*

Christ our Lord did also disco-uer to vs his *Benignity*, after a most soueraigne máner, in the Mistery of his most holy *Natiuity*. For what loue can be imagined more dear? & what communication of ones selfe more amorous? & what dew of heauen more abundant , and more

more sweet, then to see *that hidden God, that God of vengeance, that God of those Celestiall Hostes*, that *Iudge of the quicke and dead*, that *Omnipotent in his Workes,* and that *Terrible in his iudgments* ? to see him I say, become a tender and delicate little Infant, hanging close vpon the brests of a Virgin; all burning in loue, & all expiring the sweetnes, and dearnes of the same loue towards vs? And that he comes to vs, not as anciently he came to the children of Israell in Mount Horeb, with thunder and lightning, and with the terrible found of the trumpet, and with huge flames of materiall fier; and with prohibition that no man should approach to the foot of the moūtaine vpon paine of death: but that he should come to be borne an Infant, and appeare on earth, with a most clear, and sweet light

from

from heauen, to difcouer him;
and with moft delightful fonges,
and exultation of Angells ; who
being full of ioy, *fing Glory to God,*
and peace to men. And that inftatly
then, he fhould recreate, and honour thofe poore fhepheards with
an Embaffage performed by Angells; and fhould inuite them to
come vifit him, and to receiue
the comfort of his prefence, and
to be enriched with the gifts of
grace through his goodnes. And
that by his loue, and humility,
and meeknes, and fweetnes, he
fhould encourage all men to approach towards him;and to come
to him by faith and obedience;
and fo to take their part of all
the riches and benedictions of
heaué; for being the fonne of the
eternall Father,*he came full of grace*
and truth.

He alfo difcouered his *Benig-*
                                    nity

nity to vs, in the vocation of the
Magi, that firft flower of the Gé-
tiles, whom he meant to call in
after times . He calls them inftantly , as foon as he was borne,
and he fent no Prophet for them,
nor any Angell ; for they had no
knowledge of Prophets, & they
were not wont to fee Angells, and
fo they might haue rather been
eftranged by fuch vnufuall inui-
tations : but condefcending to
their condition and cuftome, he
fent them a ftarre , which by the
nouelty thereof might moue thé
to a kinde of admiration; and to
a fearch of what it might meane;
and by the fecret vertue thereof
might be teaching them withall,
that it fignified the birth of the
new Kinge ; and he admonifhed
and inuited them to feeke him, by
following that ftarre, & he gaue
them courage not to feare the ty-
rans

rant *Herod*; and he gaue thē faith
and deuotion to know, that the
Infāt, whom they faw new borne,
was the eternall God; that fo they
might dedicate themfelues to do
him eternall feruice, as to the
Kinge and Lord of heauen and
earth, whom they faw in fo great
pouerty and contempt, for as
much as concerned the world.

All this is the fupreme *Benignity*, and moft fweet dear loue of
God towards man; and it inuites
vs to feeke him; and if wee hauo
offended him, to confide, that la-
menting our finnes, we fhall obtaine pardon of him; and that he
will receiue vs, to his grace and
loue. For now, when he hath already difcouered his great *Benignity* to vs, by his facred *Humanity*;
with more reafon doth he fay,
that to vs, which anciētly he faid
by the Prophet *Ioel*, be you conuerted

uerted to your Lord God for he
is Benigne, and mercifull;and as
he is Benigne, he takech guſt in
dealing gratiouſly,and moſt liberally with you,and in pardoning
your offences paſt, and as he is
merciful he wil deliuer you from
your miſeries,and from the greateſt of them of all,which are your
ſinnes.

THE II. CHAPTER.

*Of the Benignity which Chriſt our
Lord vſed towards ſinners, and o-
ther very weake and imperſect men,
ſupporting and inſtructing them.*

A Fter our Lord had begun to
manifeſt himſelfe in Iſraell,
and to conuerſe with men,he diſcouered and exerciſed his *Benignity,* many ſeuerall waies: One of
them

them was, that such persons as
were ignorant, rude, and very imperfect, who came to demaund
succour of him, he receiued with
much sweetnes, and condescen-
ded to their great weakenes, and
tolerated their rudenes, and after a mild and gentle manner,
dispossessed them of their ignorance. *Nicodemus* the Pharisee, *Io.*
3. came to *Christ*, to be taught
by him; and though our Lord saw
his great weaknes, in that he had
not the heart to publish himselfe
for the disciple of *Christ* our Lord,
nor to confesse his faith, for the
feare he had to be persecuted by
other Pharisees, and was ashamed
that they should know of him,
that being an Ancient, and Master in the lawe, he should goe to
Christ to learne the Mysteries of
the same Lawe; for which reason
he went by night, & that in very
secret

secret manner. And though our
Lord did well discerne his great
ignorance, and rudenes, and that
he had no vnderstanding, or apprehension of spirituall thinges,
or diuine Mysteries ; but that
whatsoeuer he said, and taught,
the other did measure, and iudge
of it by the rule of corporall and
sensibles thinges, without raising
his heart from earth to the consi-
deration of things inuisible & diuine: notwithstäding all this, our
benigne Lord, did not reproue
these so notorious defects, with
seuerity, nor did he exaggerate
his ignorance, nor reproach him
for his rudenes, nor condemne
him for his inordinate feare, nor
did he driue him away for his
weakenes, nor shewed he any wea-
risomnes, or disgust in respect of
his crosse answeres; but he enter-
tained himselfe at large with him
alone,

alone , and held long difcourfe
with him, whereby he did. after
a fweet manner giue him to vnderftand his ignorance & rudenes;and he difcouered to him the
Myfteries , which were neceffary
for his faluation; namely the fpirituall regeneratiō which is made
by *Baptifme*; and the Myftery of
the *Incarnation*;which he declared
to him , by faying that he was in
heauen,whereby he fignified that
he was God , and in all places at
once. And by faying alfo that he
was defcēded frō heauē, & he fignified that he was true mā.He declared alfo the Myftery of his *Paf-
siō*,by faying that he was to be raifed vp to the Croffe,as the Brafen
Serpēt was lifted vp vpon a pole,
to the end that,as al they who beheld the ferpent were cured of
their corporall difeafes, fo might
all they be healed of their finnes,
who

who would behould and beleeue
in him, with a liuely faith. It
was a great *Benignity* to diſſemble, or paſſe by ſo many defects
of a timorous & imperfect man,
and to diſcourſe with him after
ſo louing and ſweet a manner; &
to diſcouer ſo great Myſteries, to
a perſon ſo rude and weake; and
to giue him light to vnderſtand
them, & helpe whereby he might
go encreaſing, and profitting in
the good way which he had begunne.

There came to *Chriſt* our Lord,
Mat 9 *Marc.* 5. a Prince of the Sy-
nagague, to aske remedy for a
daughter of his, who already was
at the laſt caſt, and he held her for
dead; as indeed ſhe died inſtantly
after; and he deſired our Lord,
that he would goe to his houſe,
and lay his hand vpō her, that ſo
he might giue her life. This man
coming

coming to *Chriſt* our Lord with ſo
imperfect a faith, and with ſo
meane a conceit of the power of
our Lord, as to thinke that it
would be neceſſary for the health
of his daughter, that he muſt goe
to his houſe, & lay his hand vpon
her, not beleeuing that he could
cure her without theſe ceremo-
nies; yet notwithſtanding all this,
our Lord receiued him, and conuerſed with him after ſo ſweet a
manner, and ſhewed himſelfe ſo
affable to him, that he diſſembled
the ſeeing of all theſe defects; and
he reproued him not for them,
leaſt he ſhould haue grieued him
by his wordes, whereas he ment
to cure him by his workes. Nor
did he deny that which the o-
ther asked; nor did he differre
the doing of it; but inſtantly he
roſe vp, and went with him, and
graunted not onely that which
　　　　　　　　　　　he

he asked, but a great deale more.
For he raised his dead daughter
to life in body, and he alſo gaue
health to her ſoule, by making
her beleeue firmely in him, vpon
the ſight of ſo great a miracle,
and he moued and obliged him,
to doe him ſeruice with deuotiõ,
for ſo ſingular a benefit.

This was an act of great *Benignity*, and ſo did Saint *Chryſoſtome*
obſerue thereof, ſaying; Behould
the dullnes of this man, who for
the health of his daughter, deſi-
res *Chriſt* our Lord that he will
goe to his houſe, and lay his hand
vpon her. And yet our Lord, not
looking vpon the vnworthines of
him who asked the benefit, did
with much facility and ſuauity
grant his ſuire; going preſently to
his houſe, to doe the thing which
he deſired, and much more then
he deſired. For he reſolued to raiſe
her

her from death to life; and moreouer to giue a firme hope of the
Resurrection to them, who sawe,
and beleeued that miracle.

Let vs behould other examples
of the same kinde of *Benignity*, in
his receiuing rude, and imperfect
people, after a sweet manner, and
in teaching, and comforting the,
both by word and deed . *Iohn* 4.
There came a Samaritan woman
to *Christ* our Lord; and, notwithstanding that she were a creature
of very base condition, and of
more base life; and a Gentile by
descent, and extreamely rude in
matters which concerned Religion and spirit, yet he inuited her
to haue speech with him, himselfe
beginning the discourse and desiring water of her, whereof he
knew he would not drinke; and
he fell into a most sweet and fa-
uourable communication with
her

her, and he made her a very long
Sermon, full of Myfteries, and he
paffed by the rudenes both of her
queftions and anfweres; and he
condefcended to her ignorance;
and he accommodated himfelfe
to her weakenes; and by the re-
femblance of corporall thinges
taught her things which were fpirituall; and by meanes of materiall water, he aduanced her to
the vnderftanding of the value,
and effects of the water of grace.
And he went inftructing her by
little and little; difcouering to
her firft that he was a Prophet,
and teaching her afterward, how
fhe was to honour one only God,
with fpirituall and true worfhip.
And hauing already difpofed her,
by the knowledge of thefe thinges, he plainly declared to her at
laft, that he was the very Meffias,
who was come to faue the world;

and that which he tould her in words, he imprinted in her heart, giuing her both light to beleeue it, and courage, and deuotion to confesse it.

What dearnes, what sweetnes of discourse, and conuersation, can be imagined to exceed this? That the Creator of all thinges should speake, in so familiar māner, with so base a creature, and that the eternal wisedome should vouchsaffe by his very selfe, to instruct at so great leasure and by such a lowly manner of speech, so ignorant and rude a woman, and should giue so high mysteries to be vnderstood so quickly and so clearly by her.

This is the *Benignity*, which *Christ* our Lord vsed towards this woman, and the Apostles were in wonder at it, as Saint *Chrysostome* obserueth saying; The Apostles were

were in admiration to fee that ex-
ceſſiue meekenes, and humility
of *Chriſt* our Lord, in that he was
content, ſo publickly and in ſight
of all men, to ſpeake ſo of ſet purpoſe, and ſo at leaſure, and ſo benignely with a poore woman, &
that a poore Samaritan.

There came to *Chriſt* our Lord
*Matt.9.Marc.5.*a ſicke woman who
was ſubiect to a bloody fluxe,
and ſhe came with much want of
vertue; for out of ſhame and inordinate feare, ſhe durſt not diſcouer her infirmity; and ſhee
thought to keepe her ſelfe from
being known by *Chriſt* our Lord,
by meanes of the preſſe of people, coming ſecretly neer him,
without the obſeruatiõ of others;
and meaning, after this forte, to
ſteale health frõ our Lord, without ſo much as his knowing of it,
who was to giue it. But notwith-

ſtanding ſhee came ſo imperfect and weake, our moſt pitteous Lord, did paſſe by all theſe
defects of hers, without ſo much
as reprehending them, or reproa-
ching her for them; and he gran-
ted that which ſhe deſired, and
hoped for, yea and much more
then that. For inſtantly he cured
her of that corporall infirmity,
and he cured her ſoule, by taking
away that vaine feare, to which
ſhe had bene ſubiect, and by ena-
bling her to cōfeſſe both her ſicknes, and the health which ſhe had
receiued; and by augmenting in
her, the gifts of faith and loue.
And hauing vſed ſo great *Benignity* towards her by this worke, he
was alſo benigne to her in words.
For putting her into quiet, and
giuing her comfort, he ſaid, *Thy
faith hath made the Whole*. Which
was as much as to ſay; In regard
                    of

of that faith, wherewith thou did-
deſt touch mee, although it was
imperfect, I haue deliuered thee
from thy diſeaſe: goe thy waies in
peace, and ſtill be free from the
ſame diſeaſe. So ſaith *Chriſoſtome.*
This woman had not a perfect
opinion of *Chriſt* our Lord, for if
ſhe had, ſhe would neuer haue
imagined, that ſhe could hide her
ſelf from him; & our Lord tooke
publicke notice of her, for the
good both of her ſelfe, and many
others. For by diſcouering her,
he tooke away her feare, and he
preuented that remorce of con-
ſcience, which was to accuſe her,
as hauing ſtolne the gift of her
health; and he rectified her from
that falſe imagination; and he
made her know, that nothing
could be hid from our Lord, and
then cōmēding her faith, he placed her for an example to be imi-

tated by others.

Wee alfo are to imitate *Chrift* our Lord in that *Benignity* which he vfed towards fuch as came to him full of imperfection , weaknes and ignorance; and wee muft receiue after a fweet manner our neighbours, when they come to vs full of neceffity & ignorance; enduring with a ferene countenance their importunity, & rudnes; and giuing eare and fatisfaction to their queftions; and benignely inftructing them in thofe thinges which are fit for them to be knowne by them , according to the capacity of euery one, and remouing the ignorance, wherin they are , & comforting thē with the knowledge of truth, and the hope of faluation, and appeafing their confcience, deliuering thē from vaine fcruples and feares.

To this doth the Apoftle Saint
Paule

Paule Gal. 6. aduife in thefe words.
My brethren , if any of you be
furprifed by any finne; as it hap-
pens to them who finne out of
Paffion, or weaknes, or ignoráce,
and not out of meer malice ; and
who are as it were preuented, and
furprifed by that finne , into
which they fal, becaufe they haue
not well confidered the ill they
doe , in refpect whereof they are
the more worthy of mercy , and
more eafy to be reformed; If any
fuch, I fay, haue fallen, you who
are fpiritual men, and liue according to fpirit, (that is, according
to the true and fpirituall vnderftanding of the Lawe of God) inftruct and informe well fuch a
kinde of finner as this ; and doe
it not with fharpenes, & rigour,
but with fweetnes and gentlenes
both of words, and deedes, wherin true *Benignity* confifts. And for
　　　　B 4　　　　　this

this purpose, let euery one confider himfelfe, and refled well
vpon his owne weaknes, and danger, and how fubied he is to fall,
as the other did, and peraduen-
ture worfe. And from hence he
will grow to inftruct, and correct
others, with the fweetnes of mercy, and *Benignity*, and not with
too much rigour, and feuerity;
leaft himfelfe alfo growe both to
be tempted, and conquered. This
in fubftance is deliuered by the
Apoftle; and with great reafon he
wifheth him who treateth fuch, as
haue fallen into finne, without
mercy and *Benignity*, that he looke
well to himfelfe, leaft he be têp-
ted and ouercome. For in very
truth it is the punifhment, which
he deferues, and which ordinarily
almighty God inflicts, vpon fuch
as rafhly iudge and condemne
their neighbour for committing
any

any fault, and as defpife him for
it, to let them fall into the fame
finne. As on the other fide , our
moft piteous Lord , is wont to
vfe fupreme *Benignty* and mercy,
towards fuch others, as vfe *Benignity* & mercy towards their weak
and imperfect brethren. This did
that great and admirable woman
Chriftina, with great ponderation
and feeling affirme , when fhee
faid; There is no thing in the
whole world which doth more
moue *Chrift* our Lord to vfe *Benignity*, and mercy towards men,
then to fee that themfelues are
benigne and mercifull towards
others ; and fuch *Benignity* and
mercy, cannot but leade them on
to a happy death , which will deliuer them vp to eternall life.

B 5   THE

THE III. CHAPTER.

Of the Benignity which Christ our
Lord vsed towards the Apostles,
enduring and curing their
defects.

THis very manner of *Benig-*
nity , did *Christ* our Lord vſe
towardes his bleſſed Apoſtles ,
whilſt he conuerſed with them,
in mortall fleſh . For during all
that time (which was the ſpace of
three yeares) they were very imperfect, and liued in great ignorance ; and by reaſon of their
much rudnes, made litle profit of
the great light of doctrine which
was propounded to them, and of
that ſo admirable example of the
life of *Christ* our Lord , which
they had before their eyes. Let vs
produce ſome examples to proue
this

this truth.

Our Lord had already wrought that illuſtrious miracle, in the ſight of his diſciples, *Matt* 15 of feeding fiue thouſand men with fiue loaues of bread; and ſhortly after, another neceſſity offering it ſelf, wherin our Lord was pleaſed to feed foure thouſand men with ſeauen loaues, and hauing already tould his diſciples, that he would not permit thoſe troupes of men & woemen, to returne home to their houſes, till he had fed them; they conceiued it to be a matter of ſo much difficulty, that (as if it had indeed been impoſſible for our Lord to doe) they ſaid, *where can wee be able to procure in this deſert, ſuch a quantity of bread, as would be neceſſary for the feeding of ſuch a multitude?*

What a great imperfectiō was this in them? and what a ſtrange

B 6   rudenes,

rudenes, and blindenes of heart,
that hauing seen with their owne
eyes, that our Lord had wrought
so many like, and greater miracles then that, they did not yet
beleeue, and confide so much in
him, as that with so few loaues,
he was able to feed so much people? and especially considering,
that he had declared himselfe to
haue a will to doe it; and that he
had wrought the like in the selfe
same case some few dayes before.
And yet these disciples, making
him answere with so little faith,
and indeed with so little good
manners; our most blessed Lord
did yet treate them with so great
tendernes, and sweetnes, that he
blamed, or reproued them not;
nor shewed himselfe a whit disgusted, or offended, for the little
account, and estimation which
they shewed themselues to haue
of

of his power . But paſſing by all
this , he asked them how many
loaues they had, and they ſaying
that they had ſeauen, he cōman-
ded the troupes to ſit downe, and
he gaue them all to eate of thoſe
ſeauen loaues , and he made the
Apoſtles gather vp ſeaué baskets
full of the ouerplus ; and in this
ſorte, he did by that action of his
let them ſee their rudenes, and he
remoued their ignorance, & ſetled them faſter in their faith. And
this was ſo great a fault in the A-
poſtles , that the confeſſing and
publiſhing of it themſelues, after
the coming of the Holy Ghoſt,
was an act of great humility in
them ; and the ſuffering and curing it by our Lord, with ſo great
pitty and mercy , was admirable
Benignity in him . So ſaith Saint
Chryſoſtome . It is worthy of great
admiration , to ſee the Apoſtles
ſo

ſo great friends to the truth, as
that themſelues, who wrote the
Euangelicall hiſtory, would not
couer thoſe ſo great faults of
their owne . For it was no little
one, that they could ſo ſoon for-
get that miracle, which our Lord
had wrought ſo lately before, in
the multiplication of the fiue
loaues of bread . And *Theophylact*
addeth thus ; It was not reaſon
that they ſhould ſo ſoon haue for-
gotten that miracle, whereby our
Lord had giuen food in the wil-
dernes, to more perſons, with
fewer loaues of bread. But the diſciples, were men very groſſe, and
of meane vnderſtanding ; which
our Lord permitted to be ſo, to
the end that when afterward wee
ſhould finde them ſo full of diſcretion, and wiſedome, we might
know that it was the gift of diuine grace, which cauſed it. But
their

their ignorance and vntowardnes
being fo great , as wee fee it was,
our Lord did not yet rebuke, or
reproach them for this faulc,buc
cured it with great *Ben gnny*; and
inftructed vs thereby, not to puc
our felues in choler with ignorant people , nor to be fharpe or
wayward towards them, buc that
we muft haue compaffion of their
ignorance,and inftruct them and
correct them with chatity.

Our Lord did alfo difcouer his
Benignity to the Apoftles, in that
hauing already wrought that miracle of the feauen loaues; & telling them that they were *to take
heed of the leuen of the Pharifees and
Saduces , Matt.* 16. *Marc.* 8. (which
fignified their euill doctrine and
example) they would needes vnderftand as if he had faid it , becaufe they were not prouided of
bread inough for the defert; and
fo

fo they were affraid they might
want food. And our Lord repre-
hēding this fault in them, which
they had added to the former,
faid in this manner; do you not
vnderftand , and remember the
fiue loues of bread, and the fiue
thoufand men, which I fufteined
with thē; nor yet the feaué loues,
wherewith I fed foure thoufand
men ? And thus reprouing them,
as much as was neceffary, he did
it yet in words as gentle , as you
haue heard ; and with fo great
fweetnes, as that , together with
reprehending them , he excufed
them;imputing their fault to ignorance and forgetfulnes. O admirable *Benignity*, worthy of fuch
a Lord as he , who together with
the chaftifemēt, giueth comfort;
and whileft he fpeaketh of the
fault , he giueth hope of pardon
and remedy! So doth Saint *Chry-*
foftome

foſtome obſerue. Conſider the reprehenſion which he giueth thē, all tempered with meekenes; for whileſt he reproues them, he excuſeth them; yea & he anſwereth for the very men whom he reproueth.

But let vs looke vpon ſome other examples of this *Benignity,* which *Chriſt* our Lord did vſe towards his diſciples. When thus he had anſwered that rich young man, *Matt.* 19. who ſaid. He had kept the comaundments , *If thou wilt be perfect , goe and ſell all that thou haſt, and giue it to the poore, and come and follow mee , and thou shalt haue treaſure in heauen ,* and when the young man was going ſad away, becauſe he was very rich, and had not the heart to embrace the counſaile of our Lord, and to make himſelf poore for the kingdome of heauen; Saint *Peter* ſaid

to

to our Lord, *Behould, ô Lord, how as for vs, wee haue left all thinges, and wee haue followed thee, what therfore shall be done to vs?* What reward wilt thou bestow on vs? Our Lord made them this answere; *Verily I say to you, that you who haue followed mee, shall sit vpon twelue seates, and thrones, to iudge the twelue Tribes of Israell, with the Sonne of man, when he shall sit in the seate of his Maiesty,* at the generall resurrection to a life of glory. At that day, you shal haue great authority, and glory, by raigning with the sone of man, and iudging the world together with him.

It was very little, which Saint *Peter* and the rest of the Apostles had left for *Christ* our Lord; for they were but a poore company of fishermen; and that which they had left (as Saint *Chrysostom* saith) was some fishing rod, some net,

and

and some little barke . And although together with thefe thinges,they alfo left whatfoeuer they
might growe to haue , yet that
alfo muft needes be very little;
for in the trade they had , they
were neuer able to get much.And
all this being fo little , and that
Saint *Peter* with fo much liberty,
and audacity fhould fay to him,
*Behould,ô Lord,wee haue left all, wee
had,for thee,*as if they had left moft
abundant riches and great hopes;
our Lord might with much truth
and reafon,haue faid to Saint *Peter* : W*hat greate poffefsions haft thou
left for mee ; and what great acts of
prowes haft thou performed in my feruice ?* And yet he faid no fuch
thing ; nor did he anfwere them
with any fhew of any difdaine or
euē difguft, or with little eftimation of that which had been left
for his fake; but he fpake to him
                              greac

in great earneft and with wordes,
of much weight and with fhew of
great eftimation of that which
they had left, and of that which
they had performed in following
him ; and he declared that moft
high reward of glory & that moft
eminent dignity which he would
giue them , in the kingdome of
heauen.

By this anfwere, *Chrift* our Lord
did fhew extreme *Benignity*, partly
by making fo great account of
fuch a trifle as his difciples had
left for his fake; and promifing
fuch a foueraigne reward for fuch
a fleight feruice as they had performed in following him; and
partly by fhewing how greatly
he loued them, who then had la-
boured fo little for him; and by
efteeming them fo much , who
were fo meane, and poore, as to
promife to exalt them to fo great
                              dig-

dignity, and to giue them a seate
of so great Maiesty ; and by answering them in words so serious,
so sweet , so full of comfort; and
which gaue them such a height of
hope. So saith *Origen.* Saint *Peter*
asked what reward he would giue
him for what he had left, as if he
had performed things of mighty
difficulty. But although the thinges which he & his brother left
were little , in the account of the
world ; yet in the sight of God
who regarded the loue, and great
good will wherewith they were
left, they were much esteemed.
This is the most benigne & sweet
condition of *Christ* our Lord, and
our God: who beholdeth the ser-
uices which are done him , and
the good will men haue to serue
him, & their holy desire to please
him , and that grace which he liberally bestoweth for the doing
of

of them; and therfore doth he re-
compence littleworks, with moſt
high and euerlaſting rewardes.

Our Lord, *Io.11.* whileſt he was
in the deſert, hauing heard the
meſſage of *Lazarus* his ſicknes,
and two daies paſſing on, after he
had heard it; and now vnderſtanding that *Lazarus* was dead, he
ſaid reſolutely ; *Let vs goe yet once*
againe into Iudea; for Bethania was
ſeated in that Prouince. But his
diſciples anſwered him after this
manner, *Maſter, it is but the other*
day, ſince the Iewes were ready to ſtone
thee in Iudea, and doeſt thou thinke of
going backe, where there is ſo much
danger? And our Lord ſaying ſtill,
let vs goe yet againe into Iudea, and
they ſeeing his reſolution and
being full of apprehenſion and
feare of death, *Thomas* ſaid to the
reſt of the Apoſtles, *Well then, let*
vs goe, and dy with him.

Now

Now the Apostles hauing known
by so many experiments , that
our Lord knew the secrets of més
hearts, aud that his enemies hauing a minde to take and stone
him, were not able to touch him,
because he had all power in his hands;
and hauing heard him say many
times , *that in all thinges he perfor-*
med the will , and good pleasure of his
eternall Father;they ought to haue
beleeued , that if our Lord went
into Iudea , it was most conuenient thnt he should doe so ; and
that he knew very well whatsoeuer was to happen to him there;
& that if he should haue a minde
to free himselfe from his enemies , they could fasten no hurte
vpon him ; and that themselues
going in his company , might
hould themselues secure inough;
and that without his will , they
could receiue no harme;and that
they

they ought to make themselues
wholly subiect to that will of his.
But they forgetting all this and
distrusting his power and prote-
ction, would haue hindred his
going into Iudea, and would
needes haue dissuaded him from
the resolutiō which he had taken
in that behalfe; as if he had been
either ignorant of the danger
which there he might incurre, or
impuissant in defending himselfe
from the same; and they were full
of apprehension and feare , as if
our Lord had not been able to
protect them.

And these defects of theirs being
so great, our most merciful Lord
was not yet offended with them;
nor did he shew any disgust, nor
did he reproue them with sharpe
wordes, for the meane conceit
which they had of him ; but he
informed them in sweet termes,
that

that there was no danger in his
iourney, and that they might
hould themselues safe in his company, by saying thus to them,
*Are there not perhaps twelue houres in
the day? He who goes by day, stumbles
not, becauſe the day light lets him see
the way; but he who walkes by night,
may stumble aud fall, becauſe he seeth
not the light.* Whereby he would
let thé know, that iuſt as, whileſt
the naturall day laſteth, which
hath tweiue houres of light, it is
not in the skill or power of any
creature to take away or diminiſh
any one of theſe houres, or any
part thereof; and that during this
time, a man may walke ſecurely
without ſtumbling or falling; iuſt
ſo, as long as that time of his life
was to laſt in this world, which
had been determined by the will
of his eternall Father, in which
time he was to illuminate the

C   world

world with his doctrine, and by
his miracles, there was no cause
for them to feare; for that all the
power of the world was not able
to take one moment of that time
from him; and that so both himselfe, and al they of his company,
were very safe. With this *Benig-*
nity did he tolerate their boldnes,
and cure their rudenes, and their
want of that faith, and confidence, which they ought to haue
had in our Lord.

THE IV. CHAPTER.

Of other examples of that Benignity,
which our Lord vsed towards his
disciples; enduring their imperfe-
ctions and sweetly curing their ig-
norances, and other defects.

THe two brothers Saint *Iames,*
and Saint *Iohn,* came to *Christ*
our

our Lord, *Matt.* 10. *Luc.* 22. to
demaund at his hands, the two
prime dignities of his kingdome;
and herein they serued them selues of the intercession of their
mother. Now the rest of the Apostles, seeing the pretension of
these two, grew into indignation
against them, and were offended
and troubled much, to see that
they would offer to outstrip all
the rest; and it moued a strife
amongst them, to know which of
all the company was to be the
greatest in the schoole, and kingdome of *Christ* our Lord. These
faults of the Apostles, being so
worthy of reprehésion; for faults
they were (as wee haue declared
elswhere) in some of them, of
ambition, & in the rest of enuy;
and such faultes in men who had
been so long aduised, and instru-
cted by the doctrine, and exam-

C 2   ple

ple of *Chrift* our Lord, which was
euer preaching, and perfwading
humility and charity, did well
deferue to make our Lord offended with them, & that he fhould
reproue them after a ferious and
fharpe manner, & that he fhould
punifh thē feuerely:yet our moft
meeke Lord, hauing compaffion
of their ignorance and rudenes,
which was the roote from whence
thofe faultes did fpring, vfed fo
great *Benignity* towards them,and
cured their defects,with fo great
fweetnes,that as for the two,with
onely looking vpon them, and
giuing them anfwere to that pe-
tition, which their mother had
prefented, he made them fee that
fault into which they had fallen,
by making their mother their in-
terceffour for that fuit,and by defiring to couer vnder the piety of
a mother the inordinate appetite
which

which they had to be preferred
before the reft ; and with onely
faying ; *You know not what you
aske* , he corrected and cured all
the ambition which they had ;
and fo reprehending their fault,
he did withall , excufe them by
imputing it,not to malice,but to
the ignorance of men,who knew
not what was beft for themfelues.
And as for the other ten,he reformed them alfo by calling them
to him,& aduertifing them, that
to defire commaund,and aduantage ouer others, was the vice of
Gentiles, who lodged not their
heart vpō heauēly but on earthly
thinges ; and that they were not
to doe fo , but to imitate their
Lord and Mafter, who came into
this world , not to be ferued by
men but to ferue them , yea and
to giue his life for them.

With this *Benignity,* *Chrift* our

Lord did tolerate, and cure thofe
fo great defeats of his difciples.
So faith S. *Chryfoftome*. As thofe
two Apoftles did obey the inordinate appetite of flefh & blood
and did beg of our Lord, the two
chief feates in his kingdome ; fo
alfo the other ten, obeying the
like euill inclination of flefh and
blood, were offended and affli-
&ed by the demaund, and pre-
tenfion of the former two. For it
was ill done by the two, to defire
to be preferred before the reft;
and the reft, conceiued it to be
an affront to them, that the two
fhould be preferred before them.
And Saint *Hierome* addeth ; That
our Lord, who was al meeke and
and humble, did not fharpely reprehend that inordinate appetite
of honour, wherewith thofe two
came to him ; nor yet the indignation and enuy, which the ten
con-

conceiued againſt the two;but he
treated them, and inſtructed thē,
and ured them all with ſupreme
*Benignity,*and meeknes.

The Apoſtles being in the gar-
den, with our Lord, the night of
his Paſſiõ, *he admonished them to re-*
maine watchfull in prayer, leaſt other-
wiſe, they might fall into that tempta-
tion,& tribulation, which was cōming
towards them. But they,the while,
laid themſelues to ſleepe;and our
Lord hauing been at Prayer,and
going to viſit them, and finding
that they were fallen a ſleepe,did
wiſh them a ſecond time,*to watch*
and pray;and he ſaid;Why ſleepe you?
riſe vp to watch, and pray,leaſt els you
be ouercome by temptation. And hauing giuen them this leſſon , he
returned againe to Prayer , and
after went to ſee them a ſecond
time : and finding them aſleepe
yet againe , he ſaid nothing to
them.

them. A third time he went to Prayer; and a third time he went to fee them; and finding them ftill fleeping, as being oppreffed by the great forrow they had, he faid to them, *fleepe on, and take your reft*. And fo he left them for a while, till the time was come, whē his enemies who were to apprehend him, were approaching. Then he turned towards them & faid; *It is enough: rife vp, let vs goe; for the hower is already come, wherein the Sonne of mā, is to be deliuered ouer, into the hands of finners.*

This was a great defect in the difciples, becaufe they were aduertifed, of the much danger wherein they were to fee themfelues that night; and they had promifed, that they would giue their life for our Lord; and they had been warned by him, two feuerall times in words of great exaggera-

aggeration, and waight, that
they fhould *watch and pray*, becaufe they were to be tempted in
a grieuous manner ; and their
prayer was to be the meanes, for
their not being ouercome by that
temptation . And yet notwith-
ftáding all this, they neither wat-
ched, nor prayed;and they fuffered themfelues to be ouercome
by fleepe, which was the caufe,
why afterward being ouercome
by the temptation, they fled all
away for feare, at the time when
our Lord was apprehended, and
they denyed their Mafter, who
was the head and crowne of them
all. But yet our Lord did fuffer,
and paffe by, & feeke to reforme
this fo great defect with fo great
Benignity, that finding the afleepe
the firft time, he corrected them
with no other then thefe gentle
wordes; W *hy fleepe you?* Whereby

C 5   he

he would giue them to vnderſtand, how vaine that confidence
was , which they had repoſed in
their owne ſtrength , making a
promiſe that they would giue
their life for their Lord, whereas
the while , they had not the
ſtrength to watch and pray during that little time . And when
he went to viſit them the ſecond
time , and perceiued them to be
ouercome by ſleepe, through the
great weaknes, and frailty of imperfect men , he diſſembled the
ſeeing it, and hauing compaſſion
of their infirmity, did not reprehend them, nor ſo much as ſpeake
a word , nor wake them, but ſtill
let them ſleepe . And the third
time, returning to them, & ſeing
the difficulty they had to ouercome their ſleepe , in regard of
their much ſorrow , he did not
onely paſſe it ouer, but expreſſely

                                gaue

gaue them leaue to repose and
rest, whilest he was watching, and
praying, and sweating blood for
them. With this so admirable *Be-*
nignity, and so full of the deernes,
and sweetnes of loue, did *Chrift*
our Lord treate his disciples, and
tolerate their defects, and endure
the trouble they gaue him ; and
he remoued their ignorances and
cured their faults.

THE V. CHAPTER.

How wee are to imitate this Benignity of *Chrift our Lord.*

T His *Benignity* muft wee vse
towards our neighbours, in
imitation of *Chrift* our Lord; and
especially it muft be done by Superiours towards their Subiects,
by Teachers towards their Schol-
lers , by Mafters towards their

C 6 　　Ser-

Seruants and slaues, and by Parents towards their children. Firſt they muſt exerciſe this *Benignity* by enduring their imperfections, negligences and faults; not ſuffering themſelues to be ouercome by wrath, to wiſh them any euiſſ, or to curſe them, or giue them iniurious words, or any other word of reuenge. And to this exteriour patiéce, they muſt add the ſweetnes of *Benignity*, in ſuch ſorte, as that it may be a benigne kinde of ſufferance, which ſpringeth from the interiour ſweetnes of *Charity*. To this did Saint *Chryſoſtome* admoniſh vs, who vpon thoſe words of Saint *Paul, Charity is patient, & it is benigne,* diſcourſeth thus; There are ſome who haue patience, but they doe not vſe it as they ought; for although in the exteriour, they are ſilent, and diſſemble the cauſe of their diſguſt, yet they

doe

doe it with a kinde of bitternes of
heart, yea and they shew some exteriour vntowardnes, and vnderualue of their neighbour; and so
they grow to offend, and prouoke
to further wrath, euen those very
persōs, whom they were resolued
to tolerate . This kinde of patience is not agreeable to charity
which is benigne , and vseth to
suffer with gentlenes and sweetnes both exteriour & interiour;
and whilest it is suffering, doth
not prouoke a mans neighbour
to encrease of anger, but rather
doth mitigate , and appease it.
For we must not be content to tolerate the faultes of our neighbours, after a superficial manner;
but whilest wee be suffering, wee
must also admonish and comfort
them; and thus shall we cure that
wound of wrath, which they may
haue in their hearts. Saint *Chryso-*
                                stome

Rome declareth; that this is to suffer with *Benignity.*

Superiors also who haue charge of others, muſt exercife this *Benignity*; prouiding all thinges neceſſary both for their bodies and foules: for their bodies, giuing them food, cloathing, phyſicke in their ſicknes, eaſe in their labours, and comfort in their troubles; to the end that they may beare them with contentment: and for their foules alſo by giuing them doctrine, counſelle: ſpirituall conſolation, and good example, which may edify them. This doe Prelates owe to their Subiects; Lords to their Seruants and ſlaues; and fathers to their children. *Benignity* I ſay, doth require, that Superiours make prouiſion of all thinges neceſſary, both for the body and foule, of all ſuch as are vnder

their

their charge, not sparingly & miserably, not with disgust and bitternes, and vexation of the inferiours; but sufficiently, and plentifully, according to the necessity of the inferiour, & to the ability and meanes of the Superiour; and that they doe it with facility, and suauity, and with comfort to the inferiour. For to this is the office and charge of a Superiour ordeined; not for the honour, & ease, and temporall comfort of the Superiour; but for the remedy & benefit of the inferiour, whom he hath in charge. So saith Saint *Augustine*; Wee who are Superiours, and Pastors of others, haue two capacities; the one, in that we are Christians; the other, in that we are Superiours, and rulers. Our being Christians, makes for our selues; and vnder that capacity, we are to looke to our owne profit,

fit, and good: but our being Superiours, is for the vse of others; and for the complying with this duty, wee muſt procure their benefit whom wee haue in charge. This is deliuered by Saint *Auguſtine.* And although it be true, that the Superiour, as he is a Superiour, is not to looke ſo carefully to his owne temporall profit, as to that of his ſubiect, yet doing that which he ought in his office, and complying with them whom he hath vnder his charge, he doth alſo negotiate his owne profit, & diſpatcheth his owne buſineſſe beſt, ſince he purchaſeth ſpirituall and eternall benedictions thereby.

All Superiours muſt alſo exerciſe this *Benignity*, by impoſing the burdens of their imployméts, and commaundements, in ſuch ſorte, as that the inferiours may

be

be able to carry them on , with comfort . Let them meafure out the labours , the bufineffe , and the offices wherewith they will charge their fubiects , by the ftrength, and talents of euery one of them;to the end that they may not carry them with deepe fighes, nor be forced to faint vnder thē; but that they may be able to dif-charge them with a cheerfull and contented heart . And let them moderate their directions and cō-maundments , whereby they rule and gouerne , according to the capacity and talent of the infe-riours;that fo they difpofing thē-felues to obey , and to doe their duties , may performe them with facility, and profit of their foules. So faith Saint *Chryfoftome;* If thou wilt proceed like a man who in-deed is holy, be auftere and rigo-rous towards thy felfe , and benigne

nigne and pitteous towards o-
thers: and let men fee, and heare
it faid of thee, that thou com-
maundeſt others to doe thinges
which are light, and eaſy, to be
performed;and that thy ſelfe vn-
dergoeſt heauy, and performeſt
hard thinges.

As for that which concerneth
the chaſtifement and correction
of inferiours, the vertue of *Benignity* doth not teach, that they
ſhould not be corrected: for this
vertue is not contrary either to
that of *Iuſtice*, or to that of *Charity*; both which oblige Princes
that they ſhould correct, & cha-
ſtiſe their vaſſailes; Lords and
Maſters their ſeruants, & ſlaues;
parents their children. For, the
Apoſtle faith of that Superiour,
who gouerneth the comowealth.
It is not in vaine that he hath
power and authority to puniſh;
as

as we fee by the fword he carrieth;
but it is giuen him vpon great
caufe and reafon, and for a great
good vfe; for he is the Minifter of
God, for the punifhment of fuch
as doe ill, and for the execution
of iuftice vpō their perfons. That
which *Benignity* doth teach and
exact is this; that fince correctiō,
and punifhment is neceffary, and
moft important for the generall
good of the commonwealth, and
for the particular members therof; which is, to the end that they
who are faulty, may amend; and
the reft may feare punifhment,
and take warning by others, it
muft be executed with that moderation & fweetnes, which may
carry moft proportiō to this end,
as Chrift our Lord hath taught
vs by his example.

This moderation & fweetnes,
confifteth in that, when the inferiours

riours commit fmall faultes, the
Superiours doe not exaggerate,
and enforce them too much, nor
correct them with too grieuous
punifhments; but that they moderate their wordes and deedes,
according to the fault . So faith
Saint *Dorotheus*; Be not too great,
nor too feuere a punifher of faultes , and defects , which are not
great. And fo alfo , when faultes
are comitted through ignorace,
or through great weakenes , or
vpon fome vehement temptatio,
and not with malice; obferue that
moderation , in making the re-
prehenfion and inflicting the punifhment, as that you affront not
the offender, with ill wordes; but
that the paine he is to fuffer, may
leffen, according to the ignorace
and weaknes, wherewith the fault
was made.

And fometimes when the perfon

son , who sinned through ignorance or passion , is such as that
of himselfe he growes to know
his fault , and hath much com-
punction for it ; and doth cor-
dially put himselfe vpon amendment , and that noe hurt or ill
example of others groweth by it;
the vertue of *Benignity* doth require, that the punishment be re-
mitted , or moderated at least,
very much. So saith Saint *Gregory*;Some faultes are to be punished very gently; for when men
sinne not by malice, but by ignorance, or weakenes, it is necessary
that the correction and punish-
mēt, be tempered with great moderation . And in another place;
as the fault of them, who sinne by
ignorance , may be tolerated in
some forte , so they who commit
it wittingly, and wilfully , must
be seuerely punished. And that it
is

is more conuenient to pardon a
fault fometimes, then to inflict
punifhment, the Venerable *Bede*
doth affirme fa\ing;Not allwaies
are they to be punifhed, who offend; for fometimes clemency
doth more good, both to the Superiour for the exercife of his patience, and to the inferiour for
his amendment. When faultes
are great, & vnexcufable by any
ignorance, and that it be neceffary to inflict due punifhment;
that which *Benignity* requires, is,
that the Superiour who corre-
cteth and punifheth, be not moued to it by anger and paffion;
but that in his heart, he haue
pitty of the delinquent,and that
he commit no exceffe in punifhing; but that he temper, and
moderate it in fuch forte, as that
it may not feeme cruelty, or too
much rigour: for els he who cor-
recteth,

recteth and puni.heth, will receiue more hurt, by his owne paffion, and the exceffe which he
vfeth, then he who is punifhed
will receiue good. So doth Saint
Gregory aduife, fpeaking to a Superiour. Let fuch as are good,
finde by experience that thou art
fweet towards them; and let fuch
as are euill, finde by experience,
that thou haft zeale in correcting, and punifhing their faults.
In which punifhment, thou art
to obferue this order, that thou
loue the perfon, and that thou
abhorre and perfecute the vice;
procuring that the vice may be
deftroyed, & that the perfon may
be amended, and preferued; and
according to this, let the punifhment be moderated in fuch forte,
that it reach not foe farre, as to
proue cruelty; & fo thou happen
to hurt, and to loofe him, whom
                                    thou

thou defireft ro amend, & keepe.

And to the end that the corre-
&ion & punifhment may be impofed with that modeiatiō which
Benignity requires, let the Superiour procure, that he do it not,
whileft he findes himfelfe angry,
and altered, or enflamed with
choler; but let him ftay, till his
heart be calme and quiet. And before he punifh, or reproue, let
him lift vp his heart to God,
and defire fauour and grace from
heauen; to the end that he may
do it with fuch moderation as is
fit; and to fuch end as he ought;
which is, that the delinquét may
amend, and fo others may take
warning by his example, & that
the diuine Maiefty may be ferued
and glorified by all. This doth S.
Dorotheus declare to vs, by thefe
wordes. Our Predeceffors & forefathers, the holy men, did teach
vs,

vs, that if any Superiour being
in anger, did reprehend his subiect chollerickely; in such forte,
as reprehending the other, he satisfied his owne passion & anger,
it did amount to be a kinde of reuenge; and he discouered the vi-
tiousnes of his owne heart, wherby he disedified them, whom he
was to reforme. And for this reason it is fit, that first he bridle his
owne choler, and be wholly in the
hands of reason, before he punish
other folkes.

All this moderation, which is
necessary to the end that correction, and punishment be impo-
sed with *Benignity*, the Apostle teacheth vs, speaking thus to his
disciple Saint *Timothy*; *Argue*, (that
is to say conuince such as erre,
with reasons and authorities) *and
entreate thē also.* Which is as much
as to say, admonish the good by

D   way

way of requeſt, and in ſweet manner , to the end that they may
profit; & ſuch others as are weake,
and puſillanimous , to the end
that they may get vp into heart;
and reprehend and correct the
wicked, with feruour & zeale; but
yet this you muſt doe, with much
patiéce. In a word, you muſt correct ſuch as are faulty , without
ſhewing your ſelfe angry , or in
paſſion; but let them ſee, that you
haue a calme, and quiet heart.

THE VI. CHAPTER.

Of the Benignity which Chriſt our
Lord did vſe, in touching ſicke and
leprous perſons , with his owne ſa-
cred hands.

IT belógeth to *Benignity*, to ſhew
the ſweetnes of loue, in life and
conuerſation with men . And a
                                        great

great sweetnes of loue it is, that
a man placed in dignity should
drawe neere to a poore sicke person full of soares, & should speak
to him in most amiable manner;
and should touch his soares, and
clense them, and cure them, and
comfort him with such a regalo
as this would bee . And so much
more eminent as that Lord were,
who should descéd to this office;
& so much more base as the sicke
person were , and so much the
more horrible as his disease were,
and so much the more often, and
so many more as the sicke persons
were, to whom he should vse this
charity; so much the greater, and
so much the more admirable
would this sweetnes of condition,
and *Benignity* fall out to be.

Well then, all this was done by
Christ our Lord , who being the
Kinge both of heauen and earth,

and the Lord of infinite Maiesty,
did touch with his owne blessed
hands, those poore base persons,
who were sicke of horrible diseases; and who came to him with
desire of remedy ; and he cured
them, and left them full of comfort;and this he did many times,
and to innumerable persons . S.
Luke, and Saint *Marke* relate,how
our Lord beginning to preach in
*Galilea,*after his fast in the desert,
came to the Citty of *Caphernaum*;
and being gone forth to preach
in a Sinagogue, and the euening
being already come on, all they
who had sicke persons in their
power,brought them before him.
And those sicke people , being
many . *Marke* 1. *Luke* 4. and their
diseases of many kindes,(for they
came from seuerall parts of that
Prouince , to hunt after their
health by his meanes)he touched
euery

euery one of them with his owne
facred hands, and gaue them perfect health; the whole Citty, the
while, ftanding al amazed at that
wonder, to fee how he touched
them one by one, and how inftantly withall, they were cured.

Hauing once preached a fermõ
in the Mount, he defcended towards the plaine, *Matth.* 8. *Mark,* 1.
and there came many troupes of
people to him. Amongft the reft,
there approached a mã all loaden
with leaproufy; and in the prefence of al that multitude of people, he placed himfelfe vpon his
knees, before our Lord, (but a
litle feparated from him,) and be-
fought him to cure him of that
leaproufy, faying. *O Lord if thou
will, thou canft make mee whole.* Now
our Lord could haue cured him
with the leaft word; yet, not cõtẽ-
ting himfelf with that, but to the

D 3　　　end that

that he might fhew the more *Be-nignity* , he extended his hand fo farre as to reach him , and touch his leprous body, faying , *I Will, be thou cleane*;and inftantly he was cured.

After the myftery of the *Trāsfiguration, Matth.* 17. *Marke* 9. there came troupes of people who were expecting him, and they brought a lunaticke before him , who was extremely tormented by a diuell . Our Lord commaunded the diuel to depart,who yet at his going out , did treate the young man fo ill , as that he fell to the ground like a dead body . And whereas our Lord could eafily haue cōmaunded him to rife vp, or els appoint one of his difciples to raife him , he did not fo ; but himfelfe went towards the young man,and tooke him by the ſiand, and raifed him vp; and then the

young

young man being touched, and
affifted by our Lord, who fuftai-
ned him in his handes, did rife.

Whileft he was in *Bethfaida, Marc.*
8. they brought a blind mã to him
that he might cure him, which
he would not doe in the Citty before that people, but abroad in
the field. And when he might
haue commaũded them, who led
him, to conduct him forth of the
Citty, he was not pleafed to ferue
himfelfe of any other in that office, but himfelfe would needes
take the poore blinde man by the
hand, and drew him afide into a
part of the field out of the company, and himfelfe lead him, and
became his guide, and to cure
him laid his hand vpon his eyes,
and to difcouer his *Benignity* to vs,
he vouchfaffed himfelfe in perfon, to be the leader of a poore
blinde man, which is a worke of

so much humility and meannes.
Not onely did he vse this kinde
of *Benignity* with men , but also
poore sicke woemen. The mother
in lawe of Saint *Peter* , *Matth.* 8.
Marc 1. was sicke of a violent feauer. He went into her house to visit her, he drew neer her, he tooke
her by the hand, and he raised her
vp, commaunding the feauer to
forsake her: so might he haue co-
maunded her to rise alone, but he
would not do so, but would needs
raise her vp himselfe, to discouer
his *Benignity* so much the more.

Our Lord being preaching in
a Sinagogue one Saboth day ,
Luke 13. there came before him, a
sicke & miserable creature, bow-
ed crookedly downe euen to the
ground , and tormented by a diuell; and our most pitteous Lord
called her gently to him, & made
her come neer him , and laid his
hands

hands vpon her with great *Benig-*
nity, and gaue her perfect health.

That which our Lord did with
thefe ficke and miferable perfons,
whereof wee haue fpoken, he did
at other times , with other innumerable ficke people , who were
fubiect to horrible and loathfome
difeafes, for all the world came to
him. And they who were fo weake
and wafted , that they could not
come of thefelues , were brought
to him by others, & fo they drew
neer him , and he touched them
with his moft bleffed hads to cure
the m . Now that our Lord himfelfe , fhould raife ficke perfons
out of their beds , or from the
ground, to which they were fallen, did proceed in him, from an
vnfpeakeable and moft tender
loue, who not onely was difpofed
to doe men good, but alfo to cō-
fort, honour, and regale fuch per-

fons as he did good vnto: which
was a fruite of the fupreme fweetnes of his *Benignity* and loue.

THE VII. CHAPTER.

*How the Saints haue imitated this
Benignity of Chrift our Lord towards ficke perfons.*

THis example of *Chrift* our
Lord, hath generally been
imitated much by holy men who
thereby haue been moued, & animated to ferue ficke perfons; and
to cure them, and to raife them in
their armes, and to clenfe them
with their owne hands. And this
hath been done, not onely by
meane perfons, but by principall
and great Lord; who not being
content with giuing almes to
poore ficke people, and to main-
teine them by their bounty, haue
them-

themfelues , been glad to ferue
them , and ftriue to cure them,
fometimes being ficke of leprofies, and other moft loathfome &
corrupt foares;and haue with extreme *Benignity*, done all imagi-
nable offices of charity and tendernes,yea euē fo farre as to kiffe
their leprofies,and foares.And to
the end that God might declare
how much this tender , and benigne kinde of charity was pleafing to him , he did oftentimes
concurre,by miraculoufly curing
thofe ficke perfons,who had been
touched by his feruants . Let vs
relate fome examples of this
truth.

Saint *Lewis* Kinge of France,
vfed to vifit the hofpiralls, where
there was a great number of perfons ficke of difeafes, both grieuous , and dangerous , and extreamely loathfome withall; and
D 6   yet

yet the King , without loathing
that vncleanes, & the horrour of
their difeafes , and without any
feare alfo of contagion, would go
to the ficke , and would be fer-
uing them vpon his knees , and
regaling them with extreame *Benignity* . And this he performed
with fo great cheerfullnes , and
eftimation of this office, as if vi-
fibly he had beheld the perfon of
Chriſt our Lord , in euery one of
thofe poore people. And finding on
day a leaper, whofe nofe, & whofe
very eyes were eaten out , with
the leproufy , & who was become
euen abhominable to all that faw
him; to this man he vfed extraordinary tendernes, and gaue particular regaloes , and ferued him
vpon his knees, putting the meat
into his mouth, with his owne
hands , and giuing him the wine
& water which he was to drinke.
                              The

The Count *Elzearus* of Ariano
had euery day in his houfe twelue
Leapers, & he wafhed their feet,
and gaue them meate; and not
content with what he did in his
owne houfe, he went to the hofpitalls, where they liued; and there
putting himfelfe vpon his knees
before them, he would wafh their
feet, and kiffe and clenfe and tie
vp their foares. One day in the
hofpital he found fix leapers, and
fome of them had their lips, and
mouthes fo eaté, that they could
not be looked vpon, without horrour; and the holy Count went
to them, and comforted them by
word of mouth; and afterward
kiffed the foares of euery one of
them; and this charity was fo acceptable to God, that inftantly
they were all cured, and the houfe
was filled with a moft fragrant
odour. Not onely did *Chrift* our
Lord

Lord approue this worke, by curing those leapers, who had been
touched by his seruãt, but himself
also was pleased to appeare to
him in forme of a leper, that so
he might receiue the same seruice, and regalo, which was affoarded to the rest.

Surius relateth in the life of
Saint *Ethbinus*, the Abbot, whose
feast is celebrated vpon the 19. of
October, that another holy Priest
going with him by the fieldes to
his Monastery, they encountred
in the way, a poore leper all full
of soares, and deepely groaning
vpon the ground, where he was
laid. They came to him, & comforted him, and hauing much cõ-
passion of his misery, they asked
him what he would haue? and offered him all the seruice they
could performe, although it
were to giue him of their very
flesh.

flesh. The leper said, the thinge
which I desire of you, is that because my nose is so ful of corruption and filth, you would asswage
my grief, by making it cleane.
They doe soe; and *Ethbinus* takes
him in his armes, and raiseth him
vp from the ground, and the
Priest comes, & clenseth the corruption of his sore with his toūg.
In that very instant, wherin they
beganne this worke of so great
Charity, and *Benignity*, there ap-
peered Angels from heauen, close
by the leaper, and there appeared
also a Crosse, which was placed
ouer his head; and the leaper rose
vp whole, all full of splendor, and
beauty; and they saw cleerly that
it was *Christ* our Lord. And when
he was a little mounted vp, he
said. Yea were not ashamed of
mee, in my afflictions; neither
will I be ashamed to confesse you,

and

and to admit you as my seruants, in my kingdome; and when this was spoken he vanished, and ascended vp to heauen . The two Saints were amased, and full of mighty ioy, and could not satisfie themselues with praising God, for the great fauor he had shewed them, by appearing in the forme of an poore sicke man; and for vouchsafing to receaue that poor seruice at their hand, and to reward that with so great bounty as to giue them an assured hope, that they should enioy him in his kingdome.

There haue also been many Queenes, and great Ladies, in the Church of *Christ* our Lord, who haue imitated his *Benignity*, towards sicke persons . *Fortunatus* the Bishop, relates of *Radegundis* the holy Queene of Fráce (whose feast is celebrated in August)that
shee

ſhee made an Infirmarie, into
which ſhe gathered, and wherein
ſhee cured a great multitude of
ſicke perſons, and ſhee her ſelfe
would ſerue them; and licke the
corruption of their ſoares & euen
the wormes which grew therein,
and ſhe would clenſe their heads,
& cut their haire. And eſpecially
ſhe did this to leprous woemen,
whom ſhe would embrace, and
kiſſe, and anoint, and cure, and
ſerue at table, with great ſweetnes of loue.

The Queen *Donna Iſabel*, daughter to *Don Petro* King of Arragon,
and neece of S. *Iſabell*, daughter
of the King of Hungary, who was
married to *Don Dionyſio* King of
Portugall, and who for her ſanc-
ctity, is publikely reputed and
ſerued in Portugall as a Saint
by leaue of Pope *Leo*, did not content herſelfe to giue all the goods
ſhe

ſh: had to poore people, who were
ſicke; but ſhee herſelfe would be
ſeruing and curing them, in her
owne perſon. And for this purpoſe, ſhe would cauſe both men
and woemen who were ſicke of
loathſome infirmities, as ſoares,
and leproſies and cankers, to be
ſought forth, & ſecretly brought
into her Palace, and there ſhee
cleanſed, and cured and ſerued,
and regaled them with all the ex-
preſſions of pietie, that ſhe could
make; & ſhe would kiſſe the feet,
& the ſoares of the leprous woemen. One day waſhing the feet
of a woman who was leprous, the
woman hid one of them, becauſe
it had been much eaten with the
canker and there diſtilled forth
corrupt matter, which gaue a
moſt loathſom ſauour. The Queē
made one of her woemen draw
forth the leprous foote, & put it
in

in a bafen, that fhe might wafh it.
When this was done, there came
fuch a peftiferous fauour from
that foote, that the Queenes woemen, not being able to endure it,
went all out of the roome. The
Queene remaining alone with
the leaper, did gently touch the
foote with her hand, for feare of
hurting it, and fhe cleafed it; and
ftooping kift it with that horrible
fore which it had. And *Chrift* our
Lord being pleafed to difcouer
how much guft he taketh in fuch
workes of piety, did entirely cure
the leaper at the inftant, when the
Queene kift her foote.

Now wee alfo are to imitate
Chrift our Lord, and his Saints, in
this fweet and benigne kind of
charity, towards poore ficke perfons; and wee muft vifit them in
their houfes, and hofpitalls, and
infirmaries, and wee muft ferue
and

and cleanfe, and cure and côfort
them, and prouide them, the beft
wee may, of all things neceffary.
And howfoeuer wee may be placed in great height of nobility,
and dignity, yet muſt we not difdaine to affoard ſuch ſeruices &
regaloes to poore ſicke people;
ſince this was done by *Chriſt* our
Lord, who is the King of glory;
and many Chriſtian Kings and
Queenes, haue done the fame for
loue of him. And it is a great honour and glory for vs to be able
to do a worke ſo acceptable, and
pleaſing to *Chriſt* our Lord, and
ſo profitable to our owne ſoules,
and of ſo great edification and
good example to our neighbours
and which hath the affurance of
ſo immenſe a reward in the kingdome of heauen.

THE

THE VIII. CHAPTER.

*Of the Benignity which Christ our Lord
did vse to diuers blinde men, hearkning to them, expecting them, and
illuminating them, and how wee
are to imitate him in this Benignity.*

IT doth also belong to this vertue of *Benignity*, to giue that to
ones neighbour, which he desireth, with facility and sweetnes;
yea and more then that which he
desireth; and not to reflect vpon
the indignity of him who asketh,
nor vpon the authority & greatnes of that Lord, who may need
the like; but to consider what is
agreable to charity, which whensoeuer it is great, it communicateth it selfe to all, and doth good
to all, and taketh order that in
many things, the high and lowe,
the

the great and little men of the world, be made equall to one another.

Chrift our Lord left vs many examples of this truth. Saint *Luke chap. 18.* relateth how once coming to the Citty of Iericho, a blinde man neer the way was asking almes; and when he heard the noife of the people in company of our Lord, and vnderftood that it was *Iefus of Nazareth*, who paffed by, he began to cry out and fay, *Iefus thou fonne of Dauid, haue mercy on me.* And although the people bad him hould his peace, yet ftill he continued in crying out, and befeeching our Lord that he would free him from the mifery wherin he was. Our Lord heard his cry, and deteined himfelfe in the high way, and made all that people which was in his company ftay with him, and commaunded that

they

they should bring the blind begger to him , and he stayed expecting till he came; & being come,
he asked him this question; W*hat
wouldest thou haue mee doe for thee*?
W*hat doest thou desire at my hands*?
The blinde man answered ; the
thing which I desire and beg of
thee , is that thou wilt giue mee
my sight:and instantly our Lord,
without the least delay,gaue him
that which he desired , and said;
Receiue thy sight. And he receiued
the sight of his corporall eyes, &
the sight alfo of his foule ; for
being full of faith, and deuotion
he followed *Christ* our Lord, both
with body and foule; and did not
ceafe from glorifying Almighty
God . This paffed at the entry
which *Christ* our Lord made into
Iericho , for Saint *Luke* relates
that he entred into Iericho, after
he had wrought this miracle.

Saint

Saint *Matthew* also *chap.* 20.
shewes, that *Christ* our Lord
going forth of the same Citty of
Iericho, and being accompanied
with much people, there stood
two blinde men, close vpon the
way, demaunding almes; & when
they knew that *Iesus* passed by,
they began to cry out and say,
Iesus the sonne of Dauid, take pitty on
vs. Christ our Lord did instantly
make a stand in the way, and cau-
sed them to be called to him; and
being arriued he asked the thus,
what do you aske at my hands?
They answered, *Lord that thou open*
these eyes of ours, and take this
blindenes from vs; and at the instant our Lord extended his hand
to their eyes, and they obtained
sight both of body and soule; and
they followed our Lord, being
full of gratitude for so great a benefit, and of faith, and desire to
doe

doe him feruice.

Much is here to be confidered
in the admirable *Benignity,* which
Chrift our Lord did vfe towards
thefe blind men; in that he would
hearken to their cries; and they,
being fo bafe perfons , and our
Lord fo foueraignely high , that
he would yet pawfe in the way, &
ftay for them, and make all them
alfo ftay, who went with him; and
condefcend thereby to the neceffity of thofe blinde men, and ac-
cōmodate himfelf to their weaknes . For if our Lord had gone
walking on , they not feeing the
way could not haue followed
him, or at leaft , not faft enough
to ouertake him; & he muft haue
giuen them much trouble in putting them to it. That way of Iericho, was alfo full of impedi-
ments and dangerous precipices,
as Saint *Hierome* notes ; and fo if

E　　　　they

they had been put to goe a pace
in fuch a way, they had been in
danger to receiue much hurt. For
thefe reafons did our Lord make
a ftand; as alfo becaufe he would
vouchfaffe to doe them honour,
making fo much accoũt of them,
as for their refpect to ftay in that
high way ; and to make fo much
people ftay with him . And befides , it was a great teftimony of
his *Benignity* towardes them , to
graunt them at the inftant of
their asking it; and that with fo
much comfort to them, fo great
a benefit, as it was to receiue their
fight , both in body and foule,
and fuch deuotion , as carryed
thẽ on to glorify Almighty God.

A great wonder it was, that
Iofue fhould caufe the *Sunne* to
ftand ftill , and make a pawfe in
the heauen , to illuminate the
earth, till fuch time as he had obtained

tained victory ouer his enemies;
and that the *Sunne* and all the
Orbes, which moued with it,
ſhould ſtand ſtill, obeying the
voice of *Ioſue* the ſeruant of God.
But a much greater wonder it is,
that our Lord who created both
the *Sunne*, and the whole machine
of the world, ſhould make a ſtand
in the way, obeying the voice of
a blinde begger, that he might illuminate him both in body and
ſoule, as the true *Sunne* of Iuſtice.

A great *Benignity* it is, that a
Kinge of any earthly kingdome
paſſing on his way through a
ſtreet, ſhould ſtay and make all
the Grádes of his Court ſtay with
him, vpon the cry of a begger,
who asketh almes; and that he
ſhould expect that begger till he
could arriue; and ſhould giue au-
dience to his petion; and then in-
ſtátly, open a purſe with his owne
E 2   hands,

hands, and giue the begger whatfoeuer almes he had deſired. But
a farre greater *Benignity* it is, that
the King of heauen and earth
ſhould deteine himſelfe in a high
way, and ſtand expecting a poore
begger, till he could arriue to
him, and then ſhould aske him
what he would deſire, to the end
that his owne mouth might be
the meaſure of that which our
Lord would giue him; and that
inſtantly he ſhould open the trea-
ſures both of his mercy & power,
and beſtow all that almes vpon
him which he could aske or deſire, yea and much more then he
knew how to aske.

Now our Lord by ſhewing this
mercy to thoſe blinde men, hath
ſhewed alſo a very great mercy
to all faithfull Chriſtians, inſtructing vs and perſwading vs by his
example, to vſe *Benignity* towards
our

our neighbours , giuing eare to
the cry of the poore, and beſtow-
ing with liberality , what they
aske according to the ability wee
haue: and that when they are not
able to come to vs , to aske remedy as being hindred, either by
infirmity or ignorance , or any
other weakenes, wee goe to ſeeke
them out, or make the be ſought;
to the end that wee may helpe
them, accommodating our ſelues
to their impotécy, and neceſſity.
And teaching vs alſo by this example, that wee muſt expect, and
ſtay for our neighbours , when
there is occaſió to do them good,
and to giue them comfort ; and
that although wee may be placed in high eſtate , and they in
lowe, wee muſt not yet diſdaine
to vſe this charity, and ſweetnes
towards them . And that when
our neighbours make vs expect ↄ

while , and come not so soone as
wee desire ; wee must not yet be
angry with them , nor loose the
peace of our heart; but wee must
endure with patience, and expect
and speake to them with *Benignity*, in imitation of this example
of *Christ* our Lord.

THE IX. CHAPTER.

*Of the Benignity which Christ our
Lord shewed to little children;
and what he taught vs
thereby.*

THe parents of little childrē,
Matth. 19. *Marc.* 10. *Luc.* 18.
seeing the power which *Christ* our
Lord had to cure all diseases by
touching sicke persons, brought
those little children to him ; and
not onely them who were able to
goe vpon their owne feet, but also
their

their fucking babes , who could not fpeake nor goe, but in the armes of others ; and they offered thē to him, that he might touch them , and giue them his benediction; and they had confidence that by this meanes , fuch of thē as were ficke, would recouer their health , and they who were not not ficke, would continue whole. Their parents vfed this very often, and with much importunity, for they who had children were many , and did fo much efteeme this good of their children, that no man would want it by his will; and euery one defired to preuent his neighbour, and be the firft to get a bleffing for his fonne. The Apoftles feeing this, and conceiuing that it was a thing vnworthy of the authority and grauity of our Lord, to employ himfelfe vpon fuch a light and meane

E 4   thing

thing as this, and thereby to hinder greater matters; & thinking
also, that becaufe the exercife was
fo frequent , and vfed with fo
great importunity, and ill manners by thofe parēts, who brought
their children , that our Lord
would be troubled and vexed
thereby ; did vfe feuerely to reprehēd fuch as brought the children; and would fhake them off,
as threatening them; that fo they
might not come to our Lord. So
faith Saint *Chryfoftome*, giuing a
reafō therof. The difciples droue
away the little children, and forbad them to come to our Lord,
in refpect of his dignity, and the
authority of his perfon . And S.
Hierome, declaring another reafon
faith; The difciples thought, that
as other men are wont to be difquieted, and difpleafed , by fuch
importunities; fo alfo would our
Lord

Lord be, by the frequency and
importunity, wherby they offred
their children. And Saint *Ambrose*
addeth another caufe to this, and
faith; The difciples alfo did thus,
leaft otherwife our Lord might
haue beé oppreffed, that is; much
ftraigthened and tired, by the
multitude of people, which came
to him; fome thruftling and iuft-
ling others, by occafion of the
children whó they brought. Now
our Lord perceiuing how the A-
poftles hindred litle children fró
approaching to him, though he
knew their zeale, and the intention wherewith they did it, which
was not ill; yet he liked it not, becaufe it was not fo agreable to the
diuine fpirit of the fame Lord,
but to the humane fpirit of the
difciples . And fhewing both by
his countenance and his wordes,
that he liked it not, he called &
repre-

reprehended them saying ; *Suffer little children to come to mee, and doe not hinder them;for of such is the kingdome of heauen.* I meane that heauen doth belong , nor onely to those little children, for the purity, innocency and grace they haue;but that the same kidgdom of heauen shall be also giuen to men, who in their practise of humility, simplicity, and purity of life , will become like little children.And so for that,which little children are in their owne persons, by diuine grace , which is, to be acceptable to God, & worthy of heauen; and for that also, which they represent in others, namely to be men,who are humble, innocent, and pure whom I loue and esteem much , and embrace with my very bowells, and blesse with my gifts;therfore will I suffer them to approache to me,

and

and I will admit them to my em-
bracements, and bleſſings ; and
therefore ſee you giue them noe
impediment in comming.

Our Lord hauing thus reprehended his diſciples , he called
them who brought the children;
and making thoſe children come
neer him, he put his hands vpon
their heads; and embraced them,
and gaue them his holy bleſſing
with his hands; & with his words
he recommēded them to his heauenly Father; and he made them
partakers of his diuine grace, by
the efficacy of his benediction.

By this act, *Chriſt* our Lord diſcouered to vs his *Benignity*, and
moſt ſweet condition ; in that a
Lord of ſo great Maieſty, and
who was euer ēployed in ſo great
and high workes, ſhould deſcend
to a thing, which in all apparance was ſo poore and meane,

E 6   and

and belonging wholly to men,
who had no waighty businesse in
hand; and that he should doe it,
with so cheerfull a countenance,
and with so much gust, and sweetnes, that their parents, & others
of kinne who brought the children, should presume to bring
them so often, and so importu-
nately, and to interrupt the con-
tinuance of his discourses, and
the working of his miracles; and
to éploy so large spaces of time,
in this so meane exercise.

And not onely did *Christ* our
Lord discouer his *Benignity* to vs,
by this proceeding; but he mani-
fested it to be so great, and so admirable, that it doth incompa-
rably exceed all that, which men
can conceiue, and beleiue therof. For although it were much,
which the Apostles knew of the
Benignity, and piety, and meeknes

nes of our Lord ; yet they could
not beleiue or vnderſtand, how
it could poſſibly arriue ſo farre
as this ; but did rather thinke,
that our Lord was to diſdaine
ſuch a poore imployment ; and
that he would be troubled, and
offended by the diſquiet, and importunity which they gaue him
in this kinde. But indeed it was
farre otherwiſe with him; for the
meannes of the action pleaſed
him much ; and the time it coſt,
was held by him to be well employed; and the labour & trouble
which they put him to, was ſweetly, and gladly endured by him.

Let vs imitate this *Benignity* of
our Lord, in deſcending to doe
ſuch thinges as are poore, and
meane in the account of men,
when charity requires it at our
hands; and to treate and conuerſe
with poore, and meane people,
                          though

though wee may feeme perhaps
to loofe fomewhat of our right,
and dignity thereby; if yet it doe
import for the affifting, and comforting them, in their neceffiries,
& for gaining them to *Chrift* our
Lord, doing that which the Apoftle did , in imitation of *Chrift*,
when he faid , *I haue made my felfe
all thinges, to all men*, I haue accommodated my felfe to the inclination and gufts of all men , in all
lawfull thinges; thereby loofing
fomewhat of mine owne right &
liberty , that I might faue as
many as I could.

THE

THE X. CHAPTER.

Of the Benignity which Chrift our Lord fhewed towards wicked perfons, who came to him with a corrupt intention.

OVr Lord fhewed great *Benignity* in yeelding fo liberally and fweetly to all that, which the perfōs, who came to him, defired of him with good intention, and true defire of finding remedy by his meanes; but he difcouered it much more, in yeelding liberally to that which was defired of him, with a corrupt minde, and with a meaning to calumniate him, and to drawe fome word out of his mouth, or to note fome action, wherby they might defame him, and condemne him to death.

There came to him a man of
the

the Lawe *Luc.* 10. after a counterfeit manner , to tempt him; and
he asked him , *What he was to doe
for the obtaining of eternall life ?* but
our Lord did not difcouer his
treachery , nor reprehended his
wickednes , but graunted that
which he defired, inftructing him
with wordes full of fweetnes, concerning the truth of what he was
to know and doe , for the obtaining of eternall life.

There came a Pharifee to him,
Matth. 22. who was learned in the
Lawe, to aske him which was the
greateft commaundment of the
Lawe; and he came, with a malitious minde and not with a defire to vnderftand the truth, but
to finde matter, whereof to accufe
him. And yet he without fhewing
any feeling or difguft , either in
his countenance, or wordes, did
anfwere to the queftiõ with much
faci-

facility & fuauity, and he taught
him the truth.

The Pharisees did often inuite
him to eate with them, *Luc. 7. &*
*11. Matth.22.*not with charity, but
with a peruerse and malitious intention; which was to see if he did
or said any thing , which might
be taxed; and finding nothing
whereof they could take hould
wherewith to hurt him, they pro-
cured to serue themselues of his
piety and religiousnes towardes
the making good their ill purpose ; and therefore they inuited
him vpon their Sabboth daies,
and would place sicke persons before him ; to the end that curing
them vpon the Sabboth , they
might accuse him for not obser-
uing it . And our Lord knowing
the malice, and wicked intention
wherewith they inuited him, did
not yet excuse himselfe from
                                    going;

going ; but with great facility graunted the suite they made, & accepted their inuitation;and he went to their houses,and did eate with them,and comfort them by his presence, & illuminate them by his doctrine , and edify them by his example. And though he vsed most exact temperance in eating and drinking; yet to accommodate himselfe to them, & to shew himselfe affable, and benigne towards them, he fed vpon those ordinary meats,which they vsed. And euen this was a proofe of his very vnspeakeable *Benignity*, that coming into the world to suffer for man , and carrying such an intense loue towards the Crosse,and such a most ardent desire to abstaine from all earthly comfort, and regalo; and to take all that to himselfe , which was most painfull and grieuous, that

fo he might fuffer the more for
man, and fatisfy the diuine Iuftice more perfectly, and difcouer
and exercife that loue fo much
the more, which he carryed both
to the eternall Father, and to the
whole race of mankinde; yet neuertheles, he did in many things
remit much of this rigour at fome
times, and did both in his feeding
and cloathing, ferue himfelfe of
ordinary and vfuall things; fo to
fhew himfelfe more appliable,
and fweet towards them with whõ
he conuerfed and fed; & to make
himfelfe more inuitable by all
men, and to giue them all, the
greater hope of their faluation.
So faith the venerable Abbot *Euthymius*. It was fit that our Lord
who came to take away finne,
fhould be benigne and fweet,
and that he fhould accommodate
himfelfe to the weakenes of men

to

to gaine them for heauen, as he
did;and for this cauſe he went to
the table of ſinners,and fed vpon
their meates; though he did it in
a moſt temperate and religious
manner , as it becometh holy
men to doe . And although at
times , he condeſcended thus to
the vſuall cuſtome of men for
the winning of them; he did not
for all this , giue ouer his manner of auſtere and painfull life,
which he alſo exerciſed at certaine times ; as namely during
thoſe forty daies,which he faſted
in the deſert.

This was ſaid by *Euthymius*;wher-
by it is côfirmed,that ſo to admit
of the inuitatiô of ſinfull people,
and eſpecially ſuch as did inuite
him with a malitious minde , as
if it had been but to eate with
them , was a worke of ſupreme
Benignity, whereby he ſhewed his
                                        moſt

moſt ſweet loue ; in the ſtrength
whereof, he had a meaning to cõ-
fort and ſaue all the world.

Eſpecially he ſhewed this vn-
ſpeakeable *Benignity*, in the time
of his Paſſion . For being in the
houſe of Caiphas , *Matth.* 23. *Luc.*
22. before that Councell of vniuſt
Iudges, & they asking him whether he were *Chriſt* and the Sonne
of God or no; & our Lord ſeeing
that they asked it not with a deſire of knowing the truth, or for
the doing of Iuſtice , but onely
from his anſwere to take occaſion
of blaſpheming him , and con-
demning him to death, and accuſing him to Pilate, to the end that
he might execute that vniuſt ſen-
tence , which they had giuen a-
gainſt him. And obſeruing, that
by reaſon they were ſo wicked, &
ſo vaine , and proud , they were
moſt vnworthy of any anſwere;
　　　　　　　　　　　yet

yet neuertheles that soueraigne
Maiesty of *Christ*, the Kinge of
glory refused not to giue them
answere, and disdained not to
speake to them; but in very modest wordes, was content to declare to them, who he was by saying thus; Herafter when my Passion is at an end, the Sonne of
man shall be sitting at the right
hand of the power of God;which
was as much as to say,that he was
to raigne, & discouer his power,
and authority as he was God,
coequall to the eternall Father.
And they enducing another question hereupon, saying; *Therefore*
belike thou art the sonne of God ; he
answered also to that, saying;
your selues say that I am so, which
was to answere truth: but with
very modest, and humble words;
whereby though he gaue to vnderstand, that in very truth he
was

was the Sonne of God, yet he af-
firmed it not expreſſely, as it was
fit not to doe to ſuch as would
not profit by it , though the
anſwere had been more expreſſe
& cleer. And by anſwering them
after this manner, he alſo ſhewed
his inclination to anſwere them
more plainely , and directly to
what they asked , if they would
haue knowen the truth , to haue
beleeued it. And this he ſignified
by ſaying. If I tell you what you
aske, you will not beleeue mee;
and if I aske you any thing , to
the end that I may teach you
truth , you will not anſwere mee.

Our Lord by anſwering theſe
queſtions , which were asked by
Iudges ſo wicked, ſo cruell, and
ſo vndeſeruing of any reſpect at
this hands, did ſhew how free his
heart was from all paſſion , and
choler; ſince he anſwered with ſo
great

great ferenity, & peace of minde;
and therby he preuented that af-
perfion which they would haue
caft vpon him, if he had been
wholly filent; and he difcouered
the *Benignity* and fweetnes of his
imméfe charity towards his enemies, fince he obeyed them, who
had noe right of commaundmét
ouer him, and fatisfied their de-
mandes who were fo vnworthy of
all anfwere.

Let vs follow the example of
Benignity, which here our moft
blefled Lord and Sauiour giues
vs, and not onely let vs loue our
enemies, as wee haue already
fhewed: but let vs alfo be benigne
towards them; and let vs grant
them, what they defire when it
may lawfully be done; condefcending to their difpofition and
inclination in lawfull thinges;
and fpeaking to them humbly,
and

and modelty, and fhewing them
the loue of our hearts, and the defire wee haue to giue them guft,
and contentment, in fuch things
as are agreable to the wil of God.

This doth our Lord himfelfe
expect, and aduife vs to, by Saint
Luke faying; Loue your enemies,
and do good to them: and if they
defire to borrow money of you,
or any other thing, affoard it
without hoping after any intereft. And when there is need, giue
with a free hand, without expecting any other reward, then of
Almighty God; and fo the reward
which God wil giue you for fuch
workes, will be very abundant
and great. For you fhall be the
fonnes of the molt high God, who
is benigne, euen to men who are
vngratefull and wicked; and
though they be vnworthy of his
benefits, and breakers of his cõ-

maundments, & worthy of eternall torments, yet he ceaseth not
to doe them good.

THE XI. CHAPTER.

*Of the Benignity, which wee are to vse
to wards our neighbours, doing them
honour by good wordes ; and of the
examples which Chrift our Lord
gaue vs herein.*

THe vertue of *Benignity* , requires that a man should be
courteous, and well mannered in
the wordes , he speaketh of his
neighbour; and that both in presence , and absence , he doe him
honour by his manner of speech.
For *Benignity* maketh a man sweet
and ciuill in his discourse and
conuersation, sticking close to the
end of charity , which is a spirituall, and eternall good . And a
prin-

principall part of this sweet conuersation doth consist, in that
the wordes be ciuill and curteous; whereby wee may honour
our neighbour, according to the
quality of his person and state:
and for this reason, a man who
vseth curtesy, is called benigne,
and gentle, and he adorneth his
neighbour with good wordes.
There are men, who being gouerned by a spirit of this world, or
els by their naturall condition
(not corrected by reason,) vse to
speake of their neighbours, with
little estimation of them, & when
there is a latitude of giuing thē
a title more honorable, they giue
him the least they can, so it be
without offence to the quality of
his person. And whereas they
might treate them in better termes, they proceed in such forte,
as to shew little estimation of

F 2   them.

them, and so they trouble and greiue them. And especially they speake of their neighbours, when they are absent, in wordes which shew they make little account of them;and thereby they thinke to exalt themselues, & to make théselues more esteemed by others; but they are deceiued.For in that they do not the thing,which is required by charity, *which is benigne and sweet*, they obtaine not that which they pretend, which is to be esteemed and honoured; but they are despised, and dispraised for it. For estimation springeth from loue;and if you loue a man, you esteeme him: and so on the other side, contempt springeth from hate;and to abhorre a man, is to despise him. And so when a man is wel conditioned, and curteous in his wordes, towards his neighbours, he is generally beloued;

ued ; and for the fame reafon all
men refpect, efteeme, and honour
him : for they loue a man , who
loueth them ; and they efteem &
honour, fuch as efteem, and honour them. But when a man is
difcourteous in his wordes, and
appeareth to make fmall account
of his neighbours, he is abhorred
by all men; or if they doe not abhorre his perfon , yet they abhorre his condition, & difcourteous language; and for the fame
reafon, he is little accounted of,
and defpifed by all.

This is taught vs by holy
fcripture faying; *A fweet and gentle*
word, doth reconcile, and winne the
hearts of men, and makes the their
friends, and multiplieth others,
and doth fweeten & appeafe enemies ; *and a benigne and gratious*
togue doth abound in a good man. The
meaning is; it produceth an abū-
                 F 3   dant

dant fruite in the heart of others,
mouing them also to be benigne,
and to speake gently & sweetly,
to such as speake gently & sweetly to them. The holy Ghost saith
of the seruant of God, that he is
well mannered, and curteous in
his wordes; and this is that diuine
fruite, which he produceth in his
neighbours, to make them meek,
and *Benigne*, as himselfe is. And
of him, on the other side, who is
rude, & discurteous in his words,
the Holy Ghost also saith ; *The
stroke of a whippe, maketh the flesh
blacke, and blew ; but the blow of an
ill tongue, breakes the bones ;* that is
to say ; it doth many times hurt,
and wound the soule, in such sort,
as to cause is to fall into sorrow,
and impatience, & hatred, wherby the strength, and vigour of
that grace and vertue, which it
had, is lost. This hurt, doth a
dis-

difcurteous & vnmannerly word,
which wanteth *Benignity*, produce
in the foule of man.

Of this kinde of *Benignity* in
fpeech *Chrift* our Lord did leaue
vs moft excellent examples, in
his holy Ghofpell: They brought
him one day, a man in his bed
who was a paralitike, & breaking
through the roofe of the houfe,
they placed him before him; *Mat.*
9. and our Lord, behoulding the
faith of them, who brought him,
did him fo particular a fauour,
that he efficacioufly moued him
to a great forrow for his finnes,
and to haue faith in our Lord, &
confidence that he fhould be forgiuen. And being then in fo good
a difpofition, he pardoned them,
and fo he declared himfelfe to
doe, by faying, *Sonne, thy finnes*
are forgiuen thee. This man being
fo miferable in his corporal ftate,

and being so base of condition,
as that he might without shame,
carry his couch vpon his backe,
and being a sinfull man besides,
(for as Saint *Hierome*, notes he had
contracted his disease by his sinnes) and coming to the presence
of our Lord with the vncleannes
of those sinnes, by the waight
whereof he was oppressed (for
there they appeared to haue been
take from him by our Lord;) the
same Lord being the creator of
all things did yet call him *Sonne*;
which is a title of great sweetnes
of loue, and sheweth such equa-
lity in condition, as runnes between fathers, & sonnes. So high
a Lord, doth honour and exalt
so base a man, so farre; that in
some sort he maketh him equall
to his Angells, and Saints by giuing him the name, and title of
his Sonne. For this is the great
dig-

dignity & honour, which Saints and Angels haue, to be the sonnes of the most high God. So doth S. *Hierome*, note saying; O admirable humility of *Christ* our Lord, that to a contemptible and defeated man, without strength or health in any part of his body, whom the Priests of the lawe would haue despised, and disdained euen so much as to touch, our most *Benigne* Lord was content to giue the name of *Sonne!*

There came to *Christ* our Lord, *Marc.* 5. *Luc.* 8. a woman who had a fluxe of blood; she touched the skirt of his garment, and remained whole; and our Lord hauing brought her forth to light; and she hauing confessed the benefit which she had receiued, our Lord said publickly to her; *daughter thy faith hath made thee whole; go in peace.* He honoured her by calling her

daughter, and by attributing her
cure to her owne faith; & making
her rich with Peace, and ioy of
heart; which was an effect of the
pardon of her sinnes, and of the
grace he gaue her. And thus, by
honouring the paraliticke, with
the name of *Sonne*, and this wo-
mã by the name of *daughter*; we see
it was no particular priuiledge,
which he gaue to this, or that person onely; but that it was the cõ-
mõ stile which our most benigne
Lord vsed; honouring with this
name such meane and poore mẽ
and woemen, as came to him for
any helpe.

His disciples being poore, and
meane, and very full of defects,
at such time as he conuersed with
them in mortall flesh, sometimes
he called *Sonnes*; yea and at some
other times, he would call them,
by that diminitiue whereby fathers

thers call their fonnes , *little children* ; to vnfould fo much the
more, that fweetnes of loue wherwith he called them *Sonnes* . At
other times, he would call them
Friends; and after the Refurrectiō,
when the glory of his facred Humanity , and the Maiefty of his
Diuinity was more difcouered, he
called them his *Brothers*, when he
fpake of them to others in their
abfence . For once he faid to S.
Mary Magdalene; *Goe tell my brethren,
I afcend to my Father and to your Father.* And againe he faid to the
Maries; *Goe tell my brethren, that they
are to goe into Galilea, and that they
shall fee mee there.* All thefe are titles
of great honour, and glory; and
that our Lord fhould vfe them
towards men, who were fo meane,
and poore , and at a time, when
ftill they were fo imperfect; and
efpecially that he did it after they

had quite forsaken him, in his
Passion, was an effect of extreme
Benignity in him.

THE XII. CHAPTER.

*Of other examples, which Christ our
Lord gaue vs, of his Benignity in
the same kinde.*

CHrist our Lord, preaching
in a Sinagogue *Luc.* 13. they
placed a woman, who was defor-
medly bent downe to the groūd,
by that diuell wherewith she was
possessed. Now he hauing cured
her, they calumniated him, in
respect that he had done it vpon
the Sabboth; and he defending
his miracle, from that slander
said; Which of you will not, vpon
a Sabboth day, let your oxe, or
asse be vntyed, and carryed to the
water? If this may well be done;
how

how much more is it conuenient, to vntie the bond of sickenes, wherby Satan had bound vp this daughter of Abraham, although it were vpon the Sabboth day?

That title of the whole world, which was most honourable amongst the Iewes, and whereby they prised themselues, and wherin they gloried most, was to be called the *sonnes of Abraham*; and so vpon a certaine occasion when they were disposed to magnify this honour, they said to *Christ*; *Wee are the sonnes of Abraham*. And whereas it had beene curtesy enough towards that woman, if *Christ* our Lord had said; It had been conuenient to free this *afflicted woman,* from that misery; or to deliuer this *miserable creature* from that infirmity: he could not content himselfe therwith; but was resolued to honour her with

the

the moſt glorious name, which
could be vſed, amōgſt the Iewes,
by ſaying ; *This daughter of Abra-*
ham; this woman, who according
to the extraction of fleſh and
blood, is deſcēded of *Abraham*; yea
and in the way of ſpirit alſo; for
ſhe is an Imitatour of his faith.

When *Chriſt* our Lord receiued
that meſſage *Ioh. 11.* concerning
the ſicknes of *Lazarus*, and being
reſolued vpon his death (which
ſucceeded within few daies after)
to raiſe him vp againe to life, he
ſaid to his diſciples; *Our friend La-*
zarus ſleepes, and I will goe waken
him. It had been enough, and
more then enough, for a Lord of
ſo great Maieſty , to haue ſaid,
Lazarus ſleepeth, or (ſince he would
needes doe him honour to ſay)
Lazarus my ſeruant , or *Lazarus,*
whoſe gueſt I haue been, ſleepeth; and
with this, he had done him much
honour,

honour . Yet his enamoured
heart , could not content it felfe
with this ; but he would needes
paffe on, and fay , *our friend Laza-*
rus, which is a word of the greateft
curtefy and honour. For if it goe
for a point of high honour, to be
accounted the friend of an earthly Kinge; and for a great fauour,
and regalo to any vaffaile, that a
King fhould call him by that
name; what honour muft it be,
for a mortall man to be accounted a friend by *Chrift* our Lord,
the Kinge of heauen ? and what
kinde of felicity , and comfort
muft it be, to be called fo , by
Chrift our Lord himfelfe; and that
not in complement, but from the
very rootes of his heart ? And fo
Chrift our Lord honouring *Laza-*
rus with this word of friend , did
alfo honour his difciples; equal-
ling them with himfelfe, and making

king them his companions in the
friendship of *Lazarus*, and declaring that they were all his *friends*.

This *Benignity*, which *Christ* our
Lord did vse both in word and
deed, whilest yet he liued in mortall flesh, hath been also vsed by
him, since he ascended vp to heauen, towards many seruants of
his, to whom he hath seuerally
appeared. And leauing many examples of Saints, to whom he
hath done it, sometimes in the
forme of a childe, and sometimes
of a most beautifull young man,
& sometimes of a most glorious
person; and hath honoured and
comforted them, both with words
and deedes, of must sweet loue:
Wee will speake here, of one admirable apparition, and that of
great authority, whereof we haue
made some mention elswhere, to
another purpose; and in respect

it

it was vouchfaffed to a perfon of
very meane quality it doth fo
much the more difclofe the *Benignity* of *Chrift* our Lord, and
makes vs the more confident of
his goodnes. Saint *Paulinus* Bifhop of Nola, relateth how certaine fhips going from Sardinia
towards Italy, grew into a great
tempeft, clofe by the Iland; and
the reft of them breaking, and
finking there, one of them which
was fraught with corne, did not
fplit, but yet was extremely ill
treated by the ftorme. The mar-
riners, did all leaue her, and left
alfo in her, an old poore man of
Sardinia, who was yet no Chriftian, but had begun to be cate-
chifed in that faith; and it was his
office to clenfe, and pumpe the
fhip. When the mã obferued him
felfe to be alone, and in a fhip
which had neither anker nor
fterne,

sterne, (for she had lost all, in the
tempest:) he began with teares to
recommend himself to *Chrift* our
Lord, and to beg remedy at his
hands. He passed in this anguish,
six whole daies, without eating
any thing, and still continuing
in this affliction, *Chrift* our Lord
appeared to him in great bright-
nes and beauty, and comforted
him and fed him, and commaunded him to cut the mast, which
was the ordinary remedy, wherof
the ship seemed capable, in that
extremity. For though our Lord
was resolued to deliuer the poore
man, yet he was pleafed withall,
that he should alfo do his part. He
put himfelfe therfore, to cut the
mast; and because he alone was
not able to doe it, the Angells of
heauen helped him in it. When
this visit was at an end, and the
man had difpofed himfelfe to
                    sleepe,

sleepe, our Lord came againe and
appeared to him, and gently touching his eare with his hand, and
gently pulling it, he waked him,
and required him to goe about
the doing of those things, which
were necessary for his nauigatiõ;
and in that which himselfe could
not doe, he had the assistance of
the Angells. Another time, he
appeared to him, sitting in the
pupp of the ship, where the sterne
is wont to be; letting him see that
it was he, who gouerned her. The
good man came to the feet of
our Lord; and perceiuing, that
he vouchsaffed to be so familiar
and *Benigne* towards him; & that
he did so cherish, and inuite him
to himselfe, he tooke great courage and confidence, and bent
his head downe, sometime towards his sacred feet, and sometimes reposed it in his bosome.

Our

Our Lord departed then, hauing
both by word and deed, affoarded
thofe great fauours and regaloes
of fo great *Benignity*, to this old
Catechumenus. And the fhip,
being directed, and conducted
by the fauour of heauen, failed
three and twenty daies by fea; and
and paffing by Africke, and Si-
cily, and by the Faro of that
Iland, he came at laft to the coaft
of Lucana, which is the lower
part of Calabria. There the inhabitants did receiue him, and were
all eye witneffes of the miracle;
feeing him come fafe in a fhip,
which was all defeated, without
fterne, or men to gouerne her.
From thence they conducted the
old man to Saint *Paulinus*, who
receiued him with great loue, and
baptifed him; and whereas firft
his name was *Valgius*, he called
him now by the name of *Victor*.
　　　　　　　　　　　And

And the Saint affirmes, that this was a very well conditioned, and a sincere innocent kinde of man, and that he would recount this benefit, and apparition of *Christ* our Lord, with so great tédernes, and deuotion, that whosoeuer heard him, could not choose but weepe from the heart.

By this example, and many others, ouer which I passe for breuities sake; *Christ* our Lord hath discouered, that the *Benignity*, and and sweetnes of his condition, which he vsed towards miserable mé, whilest he liued in this world in mortall flesh, is still conserued by him, and still he vseth it towards such as will profit by it.

THE

THE XIII. CHAPTER.

Of the Benignity and curtesy of speech, which the holy Apostles vsed in imitation of Christ our Lord.

THis *Benignity* of speaking in sweet & ciuill words, which was vsed by *Christ* our Lord towards men, he commaunded his disciples in the Ghospell that they should also vse, towards their neighbours. And so when he sent them to preach to the people of Israell, he commaunded that as soon as they were entring into any house, they should instantly salute them, who were in it, saying, *peace be to this house,* desiring and begging of God, the most holy gift of peace for them all. And this was to teach them,

that

that they were to be curteous and
affable, and benigne to all them,
with whom they conuerſed. The
Apoſtles obſerued this order,
very exactly. S. *Peter* the Prince
of the Church, called the wicked
Iewes his *Brethren*, who had cru-
cified our Lord, ſaying. *Act.* 23.
*Brethren I confeſſe that you did it by
ignorance; doe penance, and you ſhall
be forgiuen.* And ſuch as were conuerted, hè called his *fellowes, and
equalls, 2. Pet. 1.* in the faith, and
grace of *Chriſt* our Lord. And the
great Euágeliſt Saint *Iohn*, called
the faithfull, *his much beloued children*. And writing to a Chriſtian
woman called *Electa*; he ſaith in
the letter, *to the Lady Electa and her
children, whom I truly loue.* And writing to another Chriſtian called
Caius, he ſaith, *to my much beloued
Caius, whome I doe very truly loue.*

But what then ſhall wee ſay of
Saint

Saint *Paule*? With what *Benignity*,
with what curtefy, and good māners, and with what regalo, did he
fpeake to all men? For fpeaking
to the Iewes who ftill continued
in their infidelity, he faith *Act. 13.*
Men and Brethren , and the fonnes of
Abrabam, to you was that word fent
from heauen, which giueth faluation.
And fpeaking to the Chriftians,
who had been conuerted from
gentility he faith, *Philip. 4. My bre-*
thren much beloued and much defired,
Who are my ioy, and my crowne. And
in another place he faith, *1. Tim. 2.*
You are my hope, my ioy, and my glory.
And fpeaking to Kinge *Agrippa,*
who was a wicked Prince, by nation a Gentile, and by fect a Iew,
he made him an exordium , full
of eftimation, curtefy, and good
fafhion, faying, *I hold my felf happy,*
ô Kinge Agrippa, in that I am to defend
my felfe before thee, concerning thofe
                              thinges

thinges, whereof I am accused by the Iewes; especially since thou knowest the customes and questions, which are amongst them; and therefore I beg thy patience in hearing mee. By these few wordes, so full of diuine sweetnes and eloquence, he made him so propitious, and gained so farre vpon his good will, as to make him gladly, and with great attention, giue eare to a discourse, and sermon full of diuine mysteries. And speaking to *Festus* the Iudge, a Gentile and an Idolater; & hauing heard this word of iniury, from his mouth, *Paule thou speakest like a madd man; too much learning hath put thee out of thy wits* (for him selfe being blind, vnderstood nothing but earthly thinges, and so the mysteries of heauen which S. *Paule* expressed, seemed madnes to him) he answered thus; *Most excellent Festus, I am not madd; the*

G   *wordes*

*wordes which I haue spoken to thee,
are full of sobriety. and truth.* What
admirable *Benignity* was this, not
to be offended or disgusted, nor a
whit altered, by such a great affront, as it was to be called, *mad
man*; and to answer with so great
serenity of minde, and so great
sweetnes of wordes, so full of curtesy, and good manners, as to call
him *good or Excellēt* who was an im-
pious Idolater? and he might say
so too with truth : for although
he were not *Good or excellent* in his
Religion, nor in that kinde of
vertue which maketh a man iust
in the sight of almighty God; yet
he was very vertuous in conuersation, and morally vertuous, and
so vsing a word of a double signi-
fication in a true sence, he honoured him as much as he could, yet
still speaking truth. The Apostle
did much declare his *Benignity,* &
sua-

fuauity by thefe examples, wherby he honoured his neighbours,
both in fpeaking to them , and
fpeaking of thē: but much more
he difcouered it, in this inftance
which followeth.

Onefimus an Infidell, & a flaue,
fled from *Philemon* his Mafter, and
came to S. *Paule* being at Rome.
The Apoftle receiued him with
much loue, and inftructed him in
the faith, and conuerted him by
the grace of *Chrift* our Lord, and
baptifed him , and returned him
to his Mafter, and recommended
him by his owne letter, wherin he
wrote to this effect. I befeech thee
for my fome *Onefimus* , whom I
haue engendred , for as much as
concernes the fpirituall life of
grace, whileft I was in prifon at
Rome , and I embraced him as I
would doe mine owne bowells.
Which fignifieth to this fence , I

receiued him with much tendernes of affectiō, as a sonne whom I loue with my whole heart, & with all the affections thereof. If thou houldest mee for thy friend , and if thou louest and respectest mee, as such an one; receiue him euen as thou wouldest doe mee , with the same affection of loue , and with the same estimation , and good vsage wherwith thou wouldest receiue mee . And if he owe thee any thing, either for hauing runne away , or for taking any thing from thee, put it vpon my account , demaund satisfaction and paiment thereof at my hāds; for I offer to pay and satisfy it all, for him. Grant my suite, as I desire it , and I will reioyce with thee in our Lord , for this good worke of thine . Make my heart glad, by doing as much as I haue asked; which is to say , giue mee

this

this comfort and this regalo, that
thou receiue and treate *Onesimus*,
as I haue begged at thy hands.

Who would not be amazed to
read, and heare thefe wordes of
Saint *Paule*? That an Apoſtle of
Chriſt our Lord, a Prince and In-
ſtructor of the world, hauing been
perſonally viſited before by *Chriſt*
our Lord himſelfe, and raiſed by
him vp euen to the third heauen;
and choſen out to iudge all the
Nations of the Gentiles, yea and
the very Angells with them, in
company of *Chriſt* our Lord; and
being ſo employed, both day and
night in preaching the Ghoſpell,
and gouernment of the Church,
as that *in his breſt he carryed the ſol-*
licitude, and care of all the particular
Churches thereof; that ſuch a man
I ſay as this, ſo venerable to the
Inhabitants of heauen, and ſo
reuerenced here on earth; fhould

take fo much to heart, and negotiate at fo great leafure, the bu-
fines of a fugitiue flaue, but new-
ly conuerted to the faith; as that
he fhould write a letter frõ Rome
to *Phrygia*, which was in *Afia minor*,
where his Mafter was dwelling in
Coloffus, and recommend him to
be receiued, to be pardoned, and
to be treated well. And not being
contented to performe this office
of charity in ordinary wordes
(which yet had been fufficient,)
that he fhould honour *Onefimus*
with termes of fo great eftimatiõ,
loue and fweetnes; and fhould recommend him to his Mafter in
termes, and with reafons, of fo
great exaggeration, as a Father
would do, recommẽding his only
fonne, whom he did extreamely
loue, to fome great friend of his.

This was the *Benignity* and curtefy and fuauity of fpeech, which
the

the Apoſtles learned of *Chriſt* our
Lord , and this muſt all faithfull
Chriſtians imitate , treating our
neighbours with termes of curteſy, and good manners; and giuing thē the moſt honourable titles, and names we can, according
to the eſtate of euery one, and according to the cuſtome of that
people amongſt whom wee liue,
in ſpeaking honorably of them,
both in preſence and abſence.

In this ſorte wee ſhall preuent
many ſinnes, which we vſe to cō-
mit , for want of obſeruing the
rule of charity. We ſhall free our
ſelues from detraction and murmuring, which is a vice through
which a man contemnes, and af-
fronts his neighbour, ſpeaking ill
of him, and recording his defects
and faults , whether it be with
truth, or with falſhood. But how-
ſoeuer this is a vice much abhor-

red by Almighty God, and very
abhominable to them who feare
him;which made Saint *Paule* fay,
*detracters, who are abhorred by Al-
mighty God*. And the wife man in
the Prouerbes, faith. *The murmurer
who fpeaketh ill of his neighbour, and
maketh a fcorne of him,is abhominable
to men*. And becaufe when God
hath abhomination towards a
finner, it is to wifh him the euill
of eternall paine ; from hence it
is,that the murmurer is fubiect to
eternall malediction, and con-
demnation, as *Ecclefiafticus chap.*
28. fignifieth, faying. *The murmurer, who fecretly fpeaketh ill of his
neighbour,and who hath two tongues,*
(becaufe in the prefence of his
neighbour he fpeaketh well of
him, and in his abfence he infa-
meth him by ill report)*is accurfed
both of God and man*; becaufe he
hath giuen trouble to many, de-
priuing

priuing them of the peace , and
quiet of their hearts ; and fil-
ling them with grief and anger , and deſtroying that agree-
ment and good correſpondence,
which they had with their neighbours.

Wee ſhall alſo deliuer our ſelues by this meanes, frō the ſinne
of contumely and reproach; into
which they fall, who face to face
giue ill wordes to their neighbours;whereby they vnderualue,
and affront them; and this is the
vice of them who want iudgmēt,
as the wiſe man affirmeth , ſaying ; *He who ſpeaketh contumelious
words to his neighbours,is a foole.* And
in another place , all fooles are
apt to thruſt themſelues into
ſuites, and ſtrifes,and ſuch other
buſineſſes,as tend towards the affronting of others ; or els to the
being affronted by others , with

iniurious wordes. And this is so
grieuous a sinne, and so worthy
of punishment, as that *Christ* our
Lord said; *He who shal cal his neigh-*
bour foole, with a minde to affront
him, is *worthy of eternall fier.*

Wee shall also thus excuse our
selues from cursing others, wherby men offer their neighbours to
the diuell, that they may be damned, or els, whereby they desire
them any other euil. Which sinne
is so grieuous, as that it excludes
men from that glory, to which
they were created, as the Apostle
signified *1. Cor. 6.* when he said;
They who curse men (desiring the ac-
complishment of that with their
heart, which they say with their
tongue) *shall not possesse the king-*
dome of God.

We shall defed our selues from
these sinnes so pernitious to the
soule, which are committed by
the

the tongue, if we be well conditioned, and *benigne* in our words; whereby wee honour our neighbours in their presence, & speake not ill of them in their absence. And together with this wee shall, by the good vse of our *benigne* speech, giue great gust to Almighty God, and shall deserue much in his sight; and wee shall winne the loue of our neighbour, making them friendly, and kinde to vs; to the end that they may willingly receiue any good aduice, and counsell from vs, which wee shall thinke fit to giue. And wee shall conserue the peace, and strength of our owne soules, yea and of our estates also for the susteining of our liues; which many times is lost, by the ill gouernement of our tongues; and finally wee shall edify our neighbours, by the exáple of our good words.

All

All this was fignified by the wife man, when he faid; *The peaceable and quiet tongue, is a sweet tree of life.* Which fignifieth that it recreateth, and comforteth the hearts of men, and giues them fpirituall life, and ftrength; and frees them from the mortall diftempers of anger, and hatred, and other paffions. And this is wrought by that man, who giueth good language, through the much gaine and merit, which they get in the fight of Almighty God. And in the alfo, who heare the good fpeech which is vfed by any man of his neighbours, worketh the like effect; for thereby they are edified, and induced towards a loue of vertue.

THE

THE XIV. CHAPTER.

How wee are to exercife this Benig-
nity, and to vfe this good manners,
towards them who vfe vs ill.

SOme Chriſtians there be, who
are very courteous, and well
conditioned towards their neighbours., as long as thofe neighbours treate them with the fame
curtefy and ciuility; but if their
neighbours faile towards them,
they alfo faile ; and then they
treate thē with the fame difcour-
tefy and difgrace, wherewith they
are treated, and they vfe the fame
ill termes which are vfed to thē.
This is no good, but an ill fpi-
rir. For, that I fhould be well cō-
ditioned towards my neighbour,
becaufe he alfo is fo to mee, is
no loue of charity, but a loue of
interreſt,

intereſt, and concupiſcence; and
that I ſhould faile in curteſy, and
good cōdition towards another,
becauſe he falles ſhort therin towards me, is not the vertue of *Be-*
nignity, but it is the vice of reuenge. That which charity and
Benignity requires, and which God
exacteth at our hands, is that although another man do not what
he ought, yet I doe; and that although another man ſhould faile
of vſing me with due curteſy, yet
that I faile not thereof towards
him. For by this meanes, it wil appeare that in the ciuility, which
I vſe towards my neighbours, I
am not moued by humane reſ-
pects; but for the loue of Almighty God: and that I pretend not
proper honour or intereſt, but
the glory of Almighty God, and
the profit of my ſoule, and the
edification of my neighbour. And
in

in this forte I being of good condition, and shewing curtesy towards him, who doth not so to me,
I shal please almighty God much
the more : for I shall moue more
purely for the loue of him, and
shall exercise more vertue, and
encrease merit, and gaine more
reward in the sight of God. For,
together with the *Benignity*, which
I shall exercise, by carrying my
felfe sweetly towards my neighbour, I shall also exercise patiéce,
and humility, in bearing with his
ill condition: and I shall exercise
more charity, by pardoning the
iniury which he doth me, in treating mee ill. This was taught vs
by the Apostle Saint *Paule* with a
kinde of heauenly inuétion; asso-
ciating *Benignity* and *Patience* in
suffering iniuries, with *Charity* in
pardoning thé: for thus he fai·h;
Colof.3.Cloathe your selues spiritually,

as it becometh iust men, and the elect of God, with the bowells of mercy, and Benignity; that so you may be affable, and sweetly conditioned towards your neighbours; *and with humility, modesty, and patience also; enduring,* for the loue of God, the ill treating and peruerse condition of one another, and pardoning also the iniuries of one another. And so also, if it happen that any one be offended, and affronted by any other, and that he haue reason to complaine, yet let him pardon it in imitation of *Iesus Christ* our Lord, who when wee were wicked, and as enemies of his had done him wrong; did forgiue our sinnes and the offences, which we committed against him; and did free vs from them by meanes of Baptisme, and Penance; without taking that vengeance of vs, which we deserued.

This

This is the ſubſtance of S. *Paules* diſcourſe, & theſe are thoſe rules of *Charity* and *Benignity*, which we are to keep, that ſo we may comply entirely with the will of Almighty God in this behalfe.

THE XV. CHAPTER.

That it is not contrary to Benignity, to reprehend wicked, and obſtinate perſons in their wickednes, ſeuerely as Chriſt our Lord did.

IT is much to be noted concerning this vertue of *Benignity*, which *Chriſt* our Lord taught vs, both by his word, and by his example; that there are ſome, both ſayings and deedes of *Chriſt* our Lord in the Ghoſpell, which to ignorant perſons might ſeem cōtrary to this *Benignity*; but which yet are not contrary, but very agreable

greable thereunto . For *Charity*,
which teacheth vs , that for the
glory of God , and good of soules, we muſt vſe this *Benignity* towards our neighbors, of ſpeaking
to them in kinde & gentle words;
the ſame teacheth vs alſo , that
when wee haue authority in our
hands , wee may vſe words ſo ſeuere,and pricking in ſome caſes,
towards publicke and obſtinate
ſinners , and who by their ill example are pernitious to others,
as may diſcouer the grieuouſnes
of their ſinnes,and may diſgrace,
and condemne them as they de-
ſerue:that ſo if it be poſſible,they
may be reformed, or at leaſt that
others may feare to follow their
ill example . And now wee will
goe declaring ſome inſtances ,
which *Chriſt* our Lord left vs of
this truth , in the holy Ghoſpell.
    Saint *Luke chap.* 13. relateth ,
                        that

that our Lord being then, as it
feemed, in Galilè, which was the
iurifdiction of *Herod*, fome of the
Pharifees came and faid to him;
*Auoid this country for Herod hath a
minde to kill thee.* Our Lord made
them this anfwere; *Go tel that foxe,
that he may fee I caſt diuells both out
of bodies and foules, to day and to mor-
row, and that the third day I shall dy,
and by ending my life giue end and perfection to thefe workes of mine.* By
thefe *three dayes*, our Lord vnderſtood the time of his whole life;
and fometimes he called that, *one
day*, and fome other times *three
daies*; to fignify the ſhortnes of
this life; and to fignify alfo, as
wee faid before, that as no humane inuention or meanes was
able to make the natural day one
minute fhorter then it is; fo neither was there any meanes to
fhorten his life, by one minute.
And

And therefore the fubſtance of what he ſaid was this. During all that time of my life, which is giuen mee by the determination of my eternall Father, I ſhall conuerſe in this world, and doe thoſe workes, for which he ſent mee; which is to teach truth, & to caſt diuells both out of bodies and ſoules, and to beſtow both corporall and ſpirituall health vpon men: and as long as this time ſhal laſt, neither *Herod,* nor any other power vnder heauen, ſhall be able to take my life from mee. But when the houre ſhall be come, which is determined by my Father, I wil offer my ſelfe to death, to giue perfect life and health to the world. Yet this I will not doe in *Galile,* but in *Ieruſalem.* For as it is not fit, that any Prophet dy out of *Ieruſalem;* ſo eſpecially is it decreed of this Prophet (who for
his

his eminency and excellency is
called *The Prophet* which is the
Messias) that he shall dy in *Ierusalem* . And as for the rest of the
Prophets, it hath ordinarily been
true, and so also it will bee, that
they haue been put to death and
are to dy in *Ierusalem*; becaufe in
that Citty, the wickednes of thē
who gouerne the people doth a-
bound.

Now *Herod*, who was called *An-
tipas* , was a very wicked Kinge,
and very scandalous . He was an
adulterer, and an incestuous perfon; for he tooke his owne brothers wife from him . He was a
murtherer, & a sacrilegious man;
for he had taken away the life of
the great Saint *Iohn Baptist* ; and
as it should feem he also went a-
bout to murder *Christ* our Lord
fecretly ; leaft the people, being
inftructed by his holy doctrine,
might

might growe to abhorre *Herods* wicked life. He was alfo a moft vaine, giddy creature; for to reward the dance of a girle, he promifed the one halfe of his kingdome, if need had been; and he paid the life of Saint *Iohn* for it. He was moreouer a falfe and diffembling perfon, for he pretended that he murdered Saint *Iohn* for the complying with his oath; whereas indeed that was not the caufe, but for the contenting of a wicked woman, and for the fetling and fecuring of his owne wicked life.

Now *Chrift* our Lord, refoluing to difcouer the authority of the Kinge of heauen and earth, and of the Lord of al creatures, which himfelfe had in his hand, for the reproofe, and punifhment of all the powerfull men of this world; and to fhew how free he was from

all

all humane feare; and to giue an
example to the Prelates of his
Church, of that holy liberty,
which in such case they were to
vse, towards the Kinges of the
earth; and to discouer also, how
vile, and contemptible, sinnefull
men are, in the sight of God, how
rich, and noble, and great Lords
soeuer they might chance to be,
and particularly meaning to declare to them, who bad him take
heed of *Herod*, that he knew well
enough all the fetches and designes of that crafty man, & that
he had no need to be tould therof by any other: I say to declare
and discouer all these thinges, he
spake this word; *Tell that foxe &c.*
Which was to say vnder a meta-
phor; Tell that crafty, and diffembling man, who by the wickednes of his life, giues a pesti-
lent odour of ill example, that
what-

whatſoeuer ēdeauour he may vſe, he can take no part of my life frō mee, till my ſelfe ſhall voluntarily part with it;as I will do,when the time ordained by my eternall Father, ſhall arriue.

Being therefore moſt conuenient, for theſe ends which wee haue touched,that *Chriſt* our Lord ſhould ſpeake with this authority of a Lord, he did yet obſerue great modeſty and *Benignity* therin. For he might well haue ſaid; Tell that wicked man,that adulterer, that murderer,and ſacrilegious perſon;yea or tell it to that diuell (for all this had fitted him, & he deſerued it well:) but *Chriſt* our Lord would not vſe any of theſe termes,but fell vpon a more moderate word, as this was; *Tell that crafty and diſſembling man, that he hath no power to ſtop the courſe of my life.*And ſo ſhewing the authority,

rity, and holy liberty which the
Prelates of the Church are to vse
towardes the great men of this
world; and diſcouering alſo, his
owne diuine wiſedome ; he did
ioyntly teachvs that moderatiõ,
wherewith we are to exerciſe that
authority and liberty.

Other examples ; which may
breed the like difficulty in the
mindes of ignorant men, are the
reprehenſions which *Chriſt* our
Lord gaue to the *Scribes* and *Phariſees* of the people of *Iſraell* , in
very ſeuere wordes , which did
greatly confound, and grieuouſly
wound them; for he would ſay
ſometimes, as *Matt.* 12. *You generation of vipers, you can not ſpeake well
being ſo wicked. This wicked & adulte-
rous-generatiõ asketh ſignes:* At other
times he would ſay , as *Matt.* 23.
*Woe be to you Scribes and Phariſees
you hipocrites.* Wo be to you, *who are*

H   *blinde,*

blinde, and guides of the blinde . And Ioh.8. You are of the diuell , and him you haue for your Father, and you cooperate to his wicked ends.

Now let vs see the myſtery of theſe words of *Chriſt* our Lord, & how they were not contrary to that *Charity* and *Benignity* , which he taught vs, but full of conformity to the ſame . And let vs alſo ſee , who they be , who may vſe ſuch wordes; and to what kinde of perſons; & for what ends they may be vſed.

The Scribes and Phariſes, who were the Doctours, and ſhould haue been the true Religious mē of *Iſraell*, were at that time , not onely wicked , but wicked they were in all extreamity, and their ſinnes were very publicke, & very contrary to all Religion . And with being ſo wicked , they yet would needes ſell themſelues for

good

good, and holy; and they accompanied their wicked life, with ill precepts, which were moſt pernicious to the people. For by their wicked life, and peruerſe directions, and with their pretences and deceits, they corrupted the manners of ignorant people; and they were blind & obſtinate. And beſides theſe ſinnes, which were ordinary in them, they harboured that ſupreme wickednes, of hindering the ſaluation, which *Chriſt* our Lord came to worke, in the ſoules of men; calumniating his moſt holy life, and attributing to *Belzebub*, thoſe moſt euident and expreſſe miracles, which he wrought by diuine power; and perſecuting him to whom they ſhould haue carryed all veneration, and exhibited al obedience, as to the true *Meſſias*; and yet deſiring and procuring by all the

H 2   waies

waies they could, to put him to
death, who came to giue thē life.

These men being such as I haue
said, it was necessary that *Christ*
our Lord, (who was sent by his
Father to giue testimony to the
truth, and to take scandalls out
of the world, and to giue remedy
to soules) vsing the authority,
which he had, of Sauiour of the
world, & King of heauen, should
reprehend vice; and that concerning publicke sinnes, he should
reprehend them publickely; and
that concerning grieuous & very
hurtfull sinnes, he should reprehend them grieuously, according
to the quality and perniciousnes
of the same: that so they, who were
faulty, might well feele the great
hurt they did; and all the rest of
the people, might be disabused,
and not haue cause to follow either the ill exāple, or ill precepts
                                      of

of their wicked Teachers and gouernours. And now that *Chrift* our
Lord might execute this fo important office for the faluation
of foules, which was ordeined to
the ends of true *Charity*, fuch reprehenfions of his were neceffary,
as might declare the grieuoufnes
of the hipocrify, and other finnes
of thofe Teachers, and the hurt
they did to the people; and the
damnation which they prouided
for themfelues, by committing
fuch finnes : and he tould them,
who was the principall Author
thereof, namely the diuell, whom
they obeyed; and the neceffity
which they had, of making re-
courfe to ftrong remedies; for
they were finnes which were inherited from their predeceffors, who
had been wicked, and they were
deeply rooted in their hearts.

Chrift our Lord, did efpecially
H 3   make

make such seuere and sharpe re-
prehensions, when they did falsly
sooth, and flatter him. For many
times, when they darted out iniurious words against him, he reprehended thē not; but answered
them with all sweetnes, shewing
his humility, and meekenes, and
teaching vs to suffer wrongs, with
patience. But when they flattered
him, he reprehēded them indeed:
as when with counterfeit hearts,
they said, *Master, wee desire a signe
of thee from heauen*; for then he answered them thus. *Matth.* 12. *You
wicked and adulterous generatiō.* And
when they said, *Master wee know
that thou art true, and teachest the
way of God according to truth.* For
then he said, *why doe you tempt mee,
you hipocrites?* discouering therby,
that he vnderstood their hearts,
and that he would not pay himselfe with their flatteries, & con-
terfeit

terfeit praifes ; and teaching all
the world , that wee were not to
take guft in being foothed , nor
to defire to be praifed by men. So
did S. *Chryfoſtome* obferue vpon
thefe wordes, *Maſter wee defire that
thou giue vs a ſigne frõ heauen.* Where
he faith , that firſt they iniured
him, faying, *he had a diuell* ; and
that then they flattered him, calling him , *Maſter.* And therefore
it is, that he reprehendeth them
with vehemency , faying , *that
they were a wicked generation* . So
that, when they affront him with
ill words, he anfwereth them with
meekenes; and when they flatter
him with a falfe heart, he giues
them fharpe wordes . Our moſt
blefſed Lord difcouering to vs
thereby , that he was free from
all paſſion ; and that neither he
was put to impatience by affrõts;
nor that he was inueigled by flatteries.   H 4   THE

THE XVI. CHAPTER.

That it was conuenient , that Christ
our Lord should vse these seuere re-
prehensions. to teach the Prelates of
his Church , how they should pro-
ceed against sinners : and how the
Saints haue been euer wont to pro-
ceed.

BEsides these reasons , why
Christ our Lord did so sharply
reprehend the sinnes of the Scribes and Pharises, there is yet another; and it is for the instructing
of the Prelates of the Church,af-
ter what manner they are to reproue the sinnes of publicke,ob-
stinate and rebellious sinners ,
which are of the more grieuous
sorte,and more preiudiciall to o-
thers; and that they are to doe it
publickly,with great weight,and
force

force of words , to the end that
obſtinate ſinners may finde how
wicked they are ; and that they
may reforme themſelues , and
that others may feare , and
take warning by their ill example; and that all ſinnes , and
ſinners are not to bee reproued after the ſame manner , but
ſome gently and ſweetly ; and o-
thers with ſeuerity and rigour,
according to the quality of the
ſinne , and the obſtinacy of the
ſinner, & the hurt which he doth
thereby to others. And that theſe
ſeuere reprehenſions , which are
made in puniſhment of delin-
quents , muſt not be vſed by all,
but by Superiours, who haue authority for the ſame;and that the
end which ſuch me haue,muſt not
be the affront, nor the trouble of
the ſinner, but the reformation
both of him, & others. And there-

fore *Charity*, which teacheth vs to
be sweet, and benigne, towards
some kinde of sinners, (because
that course is fit for the good of
their soules) the selfe-same *Charity* teacheth vs, to be seuere and
strict towardes others; because
that also is conuenient, to the
end that others may be warned,
and they reformed. Saint *Gregory*
noteth this, in these words. Some
offences are to be reprehended
with vehemency, to the end that
the delinquent, who of himselfe
perhaps, vnderstāds not the grie-
uousnes of his sinne, may come
to finde it by the wordes of him
who reprehends; and that he may
growe to feare the committing
of that sinne, which he thought
to be but light, by the very seuerity wherwith it is corrected. And
it is the duty of the Superiour to
correct with great seuerity those
offen-

offences of their ſubiects, which
are not gently to be endured;but
he muſt not doe it out of anger,
but out of a holy zeale;for feare,
leaſt if he correct not faults as he
ought,himſelf grow to be faulty;
and that the puniſhment which
was due to the offences of his ſubiects, doe fall vpon himſelfe
through his negligence. And the
ſame Saint ſaith in another place;
that their ſinnes who haue not
loſt ſhame,are to be reprehended
after another ſorte, then theirs
who haue loſt all ſhame. For ſeuere reprehēſion is neceſſary for
the reformation of them,who are
growne impudent;but ſuch as are
ſtill aſhamed of their ſinnes, are
vſually better reformed,by ſome
milde exhortation.

This ſtile, of ſeuerely reprehending the more grieuous, and
pernitious ſorte of ſinnes, which

haue been cōmitted by the powerfull men of this world, and by
the falfe guide of foules , hath
been obferued by the auncient
Saints, who were mooued to it by
the *Holy Ghoſt*; and the Saints alfo
of the Euangelicall Lawe , haue
vfed the like, being inftructed by
the example of *Chriſt* our Lord;
though it be true that thefe later,
haue obferued it with greater moderation , and more mixture of
fuauity then the former; for fo
the Lawe of *grace* requires.

The Prophet *Nathan*, 2. *Kings*.
12. *chap*. reproued Kinge *Dauid*;
and hauing firſt propounded him
a parable, he concluded faying;
Thou art that man, who hath cōmitted fo great wickednes, as to
take the wife of another: and for
this finne, the fword fhall neuer
faile to hang ouer thy houfe, as a
punifhment both of thee, and thy
                                    def-

defcendents.

The Prophet *Elias,* 2. *Kings.* 18. *chap.* hauing heard that imputation which King *Achab* layed vpō him, in thefe wordes; *art thou that man who troubleft Ifrael?* did reproue him for that wickednes, which he had committed againft God, and his Prophets; and made anfwere to him, after this manner. *I am not the man who trouble Ifraell; but thou and the houfe of thy Father, are they who trouble it : becaufe thou haft forfaken the lawe of our Lord.*

The Prophet *Elizeus,* 4. *Kings.* 3. *chap.* reprehending the finnes of King *Ioram,* who was in company with Kinge *Iofaphat,* when he defired the Prophet to obtaine of God that he would fend downe water to the army, for that it was ready to dy of thirft, made him this anfwere; What haft thou to doe with me? goe to the Prophets

of

of thy Father, and of the mother;
and if it were not for the respect
of Kinge *Iosaphat*, who is present,
for my part I would not so much
as looke vpon thee.

The man of God, who was
sent by him to Samaria, 4. *Kings.*
13.chap and found King *Ieroboam,*
who was in Bethelle, offering sa-
crifice vpon an Altar like a Priest,
did addresse his speech as to the
Altar, and thereby reprehended
him, after this manner. *A sonne*
shall be borne of the house of Dauid
called Iosias, and he shall kill those
Priests vpon thee, who are now offering
incense on thee.

The great *Baptist* of our Lord,
Matth. 3. reprehending the Scribes and Pharises & Saduces, who
came to his Baptisme, said thus
to them. *O you generation of vipers.*
You men full of the venime of
sinne, and that so inueterate, as
that

that you haue inherited it from
your Fathers; who hath forewar-
ned you to fly from the wrath &
iust vengeance of God? What wō-
der, what strange thing is this,
that men so hard to be cōuerted,
by reason of your errour and the
false opinion you haue of your
owne sanctity, should come to receiue my Baptisme, and doe penance, and so fly from eternall
damnation? And Saint *Peter*, *Act.*
8. reprouing *Simon Magus* said. *Thy
money perish with thee*; in that thou
thoughtest, that the gift of God,
which is imparted by the Holy
Ghost, was to be bought with
money. I see that thou art full of
the bitternes, and gall of sinne,
& that thou art bound fast therby to euerlasting torments. And
Saint *Paul*, *Act.*13. said to *Elimas* the
sorcerer. *O man full of falshood, and
deceit, thou sonne of the diuell, and
enemy*

enemy of all Iustice, who forbearest not to doe thy vttermost, to peruert the straight waies of the lawe of God. And Saint *Steuen* said, to the Scribes, and Pharises. *Act.7. O you stiffe necked men, and who haue not cut away the wickednes of your hearts, and of your eares, with the sword of the word of God: You haue euer resisted the holy Ghost, as your forefathers did before you.*

After this manner haue the Saints (with that authority, which they had from God for this purpose, and to comply with the duty of that office which God had giuen them) reprehēded those men with sharpe and seuere wordes, who by their wicked life, and the deceit and falsehood of their peruerse doctrine, had corrupted soules. And they were moued to reprehend them thus, by their great *charity*, in their loue to God, and

and their neighbours ; and by a
moſt ardent zeale to the glory of
God, & the good of ſoules. And it
is a thing very worthy the being
conſidered , that whereas the
Saints doe ſometimes vſe ſuch
wordes in their reprehenſions, as
haue been expreſſed, they are noe
indeed affronting or iniurious
wordes , when wee conſider the
heart , and end wherewith , and
for which they are ſpoke; though
yet they may ſeeme ſo be to, becauſe they are the very ſame ,
which paſſionate men are wont to
vſe, when they affront others, and
reuēge themſelues of their neighbours. Whereby wee may be ſure,
that theſe holy mē did not ſpeake
thoſe words with paſſion, and deſire to giue diſgrace , as theſe o-
thers doe; but with zeale of charity, and deſire to doe good. And
by this rule which followeth wee
ſhall

fhall difcerne it plainly.

If they, who reprehend their neighbours, ouer whō they haue authority, with fharpe words, in cafes when there is neceffity to doe it; if they, I fay, (abftracting from thofe cafes of neceffity, and in all things els, which they doe and fay) fhew themfelues humble, meeke and full of pitty both louing, and doing good to their neighbours, and defpifing themfelues, and fuffering the iniuries and ill treaty, which they receiue from others, with patience; wee may cleerly fee, that when they fpeake fharply to finners, they do it not out of pride, or paffion, or to put difgrace vpon them; but only out of a charitable defire to recouer, and cure their foules. For the men, who when they reproue finners, fpeake words with inward paffion, and out of reuenge,

uenge, doe the like when that is
not the cafe, & they fhew themfelues reuengefull, angry, and
proud: but holy men proceed not
fo ; but when that neceſſary occafion ceafeth, they vfe al men with
much humility, and charity;and
efpecially thofe very perfons,
whom they reprehended. Wee fee
this by the examples which wee
produced before.

Though *Nathan* reprehended
Dauid with fo great liberty ; yet
when he fawe him reformed, he
went in to him, and caft himfelfe
vpon his knees, & fpake to him,
and treated him with great reuerence. Though *Elias* reprehended
Achab fo fharpely, yet after, when
the Kinge was in his chariot,
Elias himfelfe went running before him, in his company, with
much humility, as if he had been
a meer feruát of his. And though
Eliz.eus

Eliseus confounded the pride of *Ioram* with so great a reprehen-
sion; yet instantly with great cha-
rity, he did miraculously obtaine
water of God, both for him, and
all his army.

Though the man of God did
so seuerely reproue, and threaten
Ieroboam; yet seeing that the King
had one of his handes dried vp,
he besought God with great deuotion, and obtained health for
him. Though the great *Saint Iohn
Baptist*, did with so vehement
words, declare the malice of the
Pharises, and *Saduces*; yet he did it
but by way of admiration, and
praise of the power, and goodnes
of God, who had moued such ob-
stinate, and blind sinners to make
some change of their liues; and
instantly with great charity, and
zeale, for the saluation of their
soules, he exhorted and animated
them,

them, to doe workes, worthy of
penance, to the end that their cō-
uerſion might proue ſolid and
with perſeuerance. And though
Saint Steuen did ſharply reproue
the *Scribes*, and *Phariſes*; yet inſtantly he prayed to Almighty
God for them, with a moſt ardent affectiō of loue, euen whileſt
they were ſtoning him. And
though S. *Peter*, did with wordes
full of weight, deteſt the Simony
of *Simon Magus*, yet inſtātly being
full of pitty, he admoniſhed him
to doe penance, to the end that
God might pardon that great
wickednes of his. And though S.
Paule did checke thoſe great deceits, and the peruerſe life of *Eli-*
mas, the ſorcerer, yet inſtantly he
vſed much charity towards him.
For obtaining firſt, that God
would ſtrike him blind, he would
not haue that blindnes to be perpetuall,

petuall , as the wicked man de-
ferued ; but onely that it might
laft for a while: that fo,being induced by that punifhment he
might come to vnderftand his
owne finne , and fo doe penance
for the fame.

In this fort haue the Saints difcouered cleerly,that thofe fharpe
reprehenfions,whereby they corrected grieuous finnes, were vfed
by them with great tendernes,&
fweetnes of loue;and that,whileft
in the exteriour,they fhewed thé-
felues fo ftrict , and free in their
reprehenfiõs,they did euen then,
in the moft interiour of their own
hearts,humble and defpife themfelues, as Saint *Gregory* noteth in
thefe wordes . Holy men doe not
fhew themfelues fo refolute, and
free when they reproue the powerfull men of this world, as pre-
fuming vpon themfelues, nor to
the

the end that men fhould render
and fubmit themfelues to them
through the feare of man;but the
great rectitude of heart, which
they haue, makes them vfe that
holy liberty; & euen whileſt they
vfe it, they conferue themfelues
in humility; and reprehending
the crimes of finners, with great
ſtrength of mind, they iudge thē-
felues, examining their owne
faults with great curiofity and
care, and they place themfelues
in their owne account below all
others. This is faid by Saint *Gre-*
gory. And by this true explication
which wee haue made, it remai-
neth very cleare, that the ferious
and feuere reprehenfions, wherwith *Chriſt* our Lord & his Saints
haue corrected the great crimes
of finners,are not cōtrary to that
*Benignity,*which he taught vs,but
are full of the dearnes & fweetnes
of true *Charity.*   THE

THE XVII. CHAPTER.

Of the Benignity, wherewith a Chri-
stian is to be glad of the good of his
neighbour, and to approue and praise
the same: and of the example, which
Christ our Lord gaue vs thereof.

ONe of the principall things
(besides those whereof wee
haue spoken) which belong to the
vertue of *Benignity*, and the sweet
manner of conuersing with our
neighbours is, to be glad of their
good, and to praise them ; yet
with that moderatiõ, which prudence requireth, and to that end
which *Charity* seeketh . For this
maketh a seruant of God to be
amiable and sweet , and thus he
augmenteth *Charity*, towards his
neighbours, & he groweth more
able

able to be of vſe to ſoules. For by
this meanes , his inſtruction and
admonition, will be the better receiued , and the example of his
good life better allowed : and he
will haue more efficacy to moue
others. So ſaith the worthy Doctor, and Biſhop *Guilielmus Pari-*
ſienſis . *Benignity* is the loue of anothers good ; and wee call thoſe
men *Benigne,* who as ſoon as they
diſcouer a good thing in their
neighbours, doe inſtantly loue it,
and loue him for it ; and from
hence it growes, that they praiſe,
and ſet him forth in wordes.

For the exerciſe of this vertue,
there is need of great conſidera-
tion , and much diſcretion , and
light from heauen. For as by the
vſe therof with moderatiõ, being
directed to the right end, it is of
great profit , and edification towards the encreaſe of vertue ; ſo

vsing it without moderation, and
without rectitude of intention; it
is both very hurtfull to his soule,
who praiseth, and to his also who
is praised. For this reason, Saint
Bonauenture approueth this saying
of *Seneca*, praise that with moderation, which is praise worthy; &
dispraise that, which is blamable,
with more moderation. For super-
fluity of praise is liable to re-
proof, as wel as téperate dispraise.

Well then, let vs goe on declaring the errour, which is committed, and the hurt which groweth, by inordinate praise and the
manner & intention which praise
must haue, to the éd that it may be
truly giuen according to vertue.

For a man to praise his neighbour, for that which is naught, is
a great sinne; and not onely doe
they fal into it, who praise a man
for some reuenge, which he may
haue

haue taken of an enemy; or for
hauing affrōted that perſon, who
did him iniury by ſome word, or
for hauing vttered ſome carnall
ſpeech, performing ſome actiō of
that kind: but they alſo who praiſe
ſūptuous buildings, ſuperfluous
humours & gifts, curious & rich
cloathes, delicious & coſtly dyet;
and all that which hath any tin-
cture of vanity and pride, and
the regalo of this fleſh & blood,
and the loue of the world. For all
theſe thinges, are ill, and hurtfull to the ſoule of a Chriſtian;
who, to the end that he may get
to heauen, *muſt deny himſelfe, and
imbrace the Croſſe of Chriſt our Lord.*
To all theſe flatterers who praiſe
that which they ſhould reprehēd,
Eſay chap. 5. ſaith, Woe be to them,
*Who praiſe wicked thinges, as if they
were good; and who hould the dark-
nes of errour for the light of truth, and*
I 2   *true*

true light for darkenes; and who esteem the bitter life of sinners, to be sweet; and the sweet life of vertue, to be bitter.

In like manner , it is vitious for a man to praise temporall, & naturall thinges , as if they were the greatest, & principall gifts of God; as riches, nobility, strength, and beauty of the body. For these are blessings of little value , and they make not a man to be better in himselfe, or more estimable in the sight of God: & such praise breeds much hurt to the soule, for it makes a man greatly loue and praise those thinges which he should despise, & from which he should estrange his heart . The holy scripture condemneth this vice saying , doe not praise men for the corporall beauty which they haue ; nor despise them for their poore, & meane apparance. Consider that the Bee, being but a very

a very little creature, giueth so
excellent a fruite, as that it is the
most sweet of all sweet thinges;
for there is nothing more sweet,
then hony. The meaning is, that
as the little Bee, hath efficacy to
produce such a fruite ; so may a
little body, & a meane presence,
haue much vertue . And that
which the Holy Ghost saith of
the beauty of the body, he will
haue vs vnderstand of all other
naturall, and temporall gifts,
which are of so little value, that
a man is noe further worthy of
estimation or praise for them, thē
if he had them not; but onely so
farre forth, as there may result
some profit to the soule thereby.
This was taught vs, both by the
example, and diuine wordes of
Christ our Lord. For a certaine de-
uoute womā, hauing seen his miracles, and hauing heard his do-

I 3   ctrine,

&ctrine, was not able to conteine herselfe, but that she must needes praise that *Mother* aloud, who had brought forth such a *Sonne*, saying; *Blessed is the wombe, which bare thee, and the brests which gaue thee sucke* . But *Christ* our Lord gaue her this answere; *Nay, rather blessed are they who heare the word of God, and keepe it* . By which wordes he discouered to vs, how that free & gratuite blessing, whereby the most sacred Virgin was made Mother of the naturall Sonne of God, did not alone, and of it selfe make her happy or blessed, nor worthy of the reward of heauen: nor more great in the sight of God; but the vnspeakeable vertue, and suauity, and grace, wherby Almighty God did exalt, and dignify her, for such an office: & that which afterward he gaue her, in regard of so high a dignity,

nity, was the thing which made
her fo truly happy.

If then fo admirable a gift, as
that was, did not deferue great
praife for it felfe alone, but for
that vertue and fanctity which
went in company thereof: how
much more, muft all temporall
bleffings, and gifts of nature,
which in themfelues are fo poore
and perifhing, be vnworthy of
praife; but onely fo farre forth, as
they may be found to affift, and
concurre towards the good of the
foule?

So faith Saint *Chryfoftome*, declaring thefe wordes of *Chrift* our
Lord. By this fentence, *Chrift* our
Lord did make vs know, that it
would not haue profited the *Vir-*
gin, to haue brought forth the
Sonne of God, if fhee had not
withall, been endowed with that
faith, and incomparable fanctity

which shee had. And therefore, as
I said, if so great a dignity, would
not haue profited the *blessed Virgin*,
without the vertue, and sanctity
of her foule; how much more
clear is it, that it will serue vs to
little purpofe, before Almighty
God, to haue Saints to our Fathers, or fonnes, or kinred, or fuch
other externall gifts; if withall,
wee haue not goodnes and vertue, and doe not lead a fpirituall
life? For this is that which maketh men to be of value, & worthy of praife, in the fight of God.

It is also an errour, and fault
of flattery, to praife our neighbour for any vertue, which he
may haue, and thereby to delight
and comfort him principally, for
the temporall gaine and profit,
which he hopeth to receiue of
him. For the praife of true vertue, which principally is to be ordeined

deined to fome fpirituall good,
and to the feruice of God, is or-
deined by him to his owne priuate interest, which is a finnefull
thing; & fo much the more grieuous it will be , as there is more
inordinatenes in the thing. And
when it is very great,that will be
fulfilled in their perfons; which
is fpoken of by the Pfalmift,*Pfal.*
2. God will defeate and deftroy,
the ftrength and authority of
them, who defire and procure to
pleafe,and giue guft to men:and
haue that for their end,not looking vp towards God , but downe
vpon their owne priuate intereft
and humour.Efpecially they who
procure to pleafe worldly men,
forbearing to doe thofe thinges
which they owe to God,in refpect
of them : thefe indeed , fhall be
confounded , and put to fhame,
by Almighty God. For both in

this life, euen all their temporall
hopes shall prooue vaine; and besides, in the other life, they shall
be fulfilled with shame, and deliuered ouer to eternall torments.

Besides it is a defect, and the
fault of soothing, to praise a man
either for his wit, or learning, or
for the talents, and parts which
he hath: yea or euen for his true
vertue; when it is likely, that
through his weakenes, or vnmor-
tified ill inclination he may fall
into pride, and vaine complacéce
in himself, or into any other preiudice of his soule. Saint *Augustine*
obserued this, in these wordes. A
hard thing it is, that some little
impurity of errour, doe not stick
to the hart of a man, (euē though
it be cleane) vpon the praises of
another; vnles indeed he should
haue it so very cleane, as that he
should take no gust in them, nor
be

be touched by any vapour of the;
and vnlès the praiſe which they
giue him, ſhould more content
him for the good of them, who
praiſe him, then for the comforr,
or honour, or eſtimation, which
may growe thereby to himſelfe.
And thē he may know, that their
praiſe of him, is profitable to thē,
if in their life they honour not
him, but God; nor faſtning their
mindes vpon him, by the praiſe,
& honour, which they giue him,
but riſing vp by him, towards Almighty God, whoſe moſt ſacred
temple euery man is, who liueth
well. So that it may be fulfilled
in him, which is ſpoken of, by the
Pſalmiſt; My ſoule ſhall be praiſed by ſuch, as are good; not in it
ſelfe but in our Lord; that is to
ſay, for the gifts which it hath of
our Lord, and for the glory of the
ſame Lord.

I 6 This

This is the danger to which they are ordinarily subiect, who are much praised by men; vnles they be possessors of true and solid vertue, whereby they may resist vaine complacence, and refer the praise to the Author of all good thinges, which is God. For so saith the holy Scripture; *Better is it , to be corrected by a discreet and wise man, then to be praised by an imprudent man , who with his smooth kinde of praising leaues vs in errour.* And declaring the danger wherin man is , when he who praiseth, doth not obserue the moderatiõ, and end which ought to be kept. Saint *Hierome* said ; There is nothing which doth so easily infect, and corrupt the hearts of men as flattery; and the tongue of a flatterer doth more hurt , then the sword of a persecutour.

Another fault is also committed

ted

ted in praising some, when it is
for the dispraise of others. A man
will not dare expressely to speake
ill of his neighbour, especially to
one who hath auersion from hearing it;and therefore to doe it the
more couertly, he doth it by
meanes of praising another man
for the same vertues and gifts
of his, and then the detracter
would haue it thought, that the
man whom he meaneth to dif-
praise, doth want those vertues,
or else is subiect to the contrary
defects. Saint *Chrysostome* noteth
this vice, in these wordes: We doe
many good thinges; but not allwaies with a good minde. Wee
praise many; but not to the end,
that we may speake well of them,
but to detract and speake ill of
others. Now that which wee say
is good, because we praise vertue
in another; but the minde, wherwith

with wee fay it, is infected with
finne, and fet on worke by Satan:
for wee pretend not to doe him
good, whom wee praife, but hurt
to him whom wee difpraife.

These are the defects, and vi-
ces, which growe by praifinge o-
thers, when it is done without
difcretion and moderation; and
without that end to which it
ought to be addreffed; and fo it
leaueth to be vertue, as is turned
into the vice of flattery. And now
wee will declare, how praife is to
be vfed, to the end that it may be
a fruite of the vertue of *Charity* &
Benignity. And wee will produce
fome examples, which *Chrift* our
Lord fhewed vs, concerning the
manner and intention, which we
were to hould in praifinge our
neighbours,

THE

THE XVIII. CHAPTER.

Of the intention, and moderatiõ, wher-
with we are to praise vertue in our
neighbours : and of the examples
which Christ our Lord gaue vs
thereof.

IT is a thing both lawfull and
very pleasing to Almighty
God, for a man to praise his
neighbours, for the good he hath
done; to the end that being praised, they may loue vertue so much
the more, and be animated to the
exercise thereof; and not be dis-
maied by the troubles, and difficulties, to which a vertuous life
is subiect. And this is principally
to be done, towards men, who
are but beginners in the way of
vertue; and who are weake, and
of little heart; for such persons
                                haue

haue the greater need of helpe.
Yet euen this praise muſt be giuen with the moderation aforeſaid; in ſuch ſort, as that it may
profit, and not hurt the party
praiſed; but may edify, and induce him to a loue and eſtimation of vertue, and not to a preſumption in himſelfe, and a loue
of vanity. For the obtaining of
this end, the praiſe muſt be giuen
in words; which may not greatly
exaggerate, or amplify the vertue; but plainly declare the truth,
and his approbation thereof. Let
vs ſee ſome exáples, which *Chriſt*
our Lord gaue of this. *Nathaniell*
came to *Chriſt* our Lord, *Iohn* 1.
being brought to him by Saint
Philip. This *Nathaniell*, was a man
full of vertue, & very obſeruant
of the lawe; and came in doubt,
whether or no *Chriſt* our Lord
were the true *Meſſias*, as S. *Philip*
had

had said he was. And drawing,
neer, our Lord looked vpon his
diſciples, and ſaid in the hearing
of *Nathaniell* : *Behould here a true
Iſraelite , in whom there is no guile.*
As if he had ſaid; Behould here a
man truly good, not diſſembling
or counterfeit ; but that vertue
which he ſheweth in his exteriour faſhion, and publicke conuerſation, which is ſubiect to the
ſight of men, is poſſeſt by him in
the ſecret, & moſt interiour part
of his heart, which is ſeen by Almighty God.

This was a true, and moderate
praiſe, and much good grew to
Nathaniell by it; for therby he vn-
ſtood, that *Chriſt* our Lord knew
the ſecrets of his heart, and he was
certified of it ſo much the more,
by the further anſwere of *Chriſt*
our Lord. For ſaying to him,
where knew you mee ? he anſwered,
I ſawe

*I saw thee, when thou wert vnder the
figtree.*It should seem that *Nathaniell* , had retired himselfe vnder
that tree to pray, or to doe some
other good worke ; and so he in-
ferring thereby , (as a wise man
might well doe,) that *Christ* our
Lord knew all thinges, he beleeued perfectly in him, and tooke
him for his Master. Let vs deliuer another example of the same
truth.

  Christ our Lord, *Luke* 19. came
into the house of *Zaccheus* the Pu-
blican ; and he mooued him by
his wordes, and by his presence,
to so great pennance, and change
of life:that not onely he resolued
to giue ouer all those sinnes into
which he had fallen, & to restore
all that, to the restitution wherof
he was obliged ; but to render it
foure fould ; thereby giuing satisfaction for the fault he had
                    com-

mitted , by voluntarily vnder-
going the paine, which the lawe
impofed vpon fuch perfons , as
tooke away the goods of others;
and befides all this, he gaue halfe
his fubftance to the poore. *Chrift*
our Lord perceiuing fo good be-
ginnings of a holy life in *Zac-*
cheus, did praife him : by faying
of him , to the ftanders by ; *This*
day, is true faluation wrought in this
houfe; For the Mafter and owner
of it , is already a true fonne of
Abraham:not only now by the extraction of flefh and blood ; but
by the imitation of his faith,and
vertue . In this forte therefore,
did *Chrift* our Lord praife *Natha-*
niell, who was a new beginner in
his fchoole of vertue and good
life, and fo alfo did he praife *Zac-*
cheus. And the praife was true,and
moderate; & it did no more then
declare in plaine wordes,that the
one

one of them, was a man truly
good, and the other truly peni-
tent & by meanes of thefe words,
he ftrengthned and encouraged
them, both to perfeuer and grow
in the good courfe which they
had begunne.

But not only did *Chrift* our Lord
praife them, who had good in-
tentions,& who were truly good;
and vpright and well meaninge
foules, as *Nathaniell* already was
before, and *Zacchaus* was growne
to be; but he approued,and praifed alfo that good which was faid,
or done, by fuch as came to him,
euen with an ill minde. There
came a man, *Luc.10.* who was learned in the Lawe, to tempt him,
asking *what he was to doe, for the
obtaining of eternall life?* Chrift our
Lord demaunded of him, *how it
was written in the Lawe?* He anfwered, *It is written that thou shalt loue*
                                    the

*the Lord thy God with all thy heart,
and thy neighbour as thy selfe* . Our
Lord thē faid to him, (by way of
allowing & praifing what he had
formerly faid;) *Thou haſt anſwered
well: doe as thou haſt faid , and as the
Lawe commaundeth , and thou shalt
obtaine euerlaſting life.*

There came , another time , a
Pharify to our Lord, *Mat 22 Marc.*
12. in name of all the reſt , to fee
if he could draw fome fuch anfwere from him , as whereby he
might calumniate him ; and he
asked him , *which was the greateſt
commaundment of the law?* And *Chriſt*
our Lord , hauing anfwered him,
*that it was to loue God with all the
heart* ; the Pharify approued the
anfwere of our Lord , and added
thereunto thefe words: *that to loue
God with all the heart, and the neighbour as ones felfe, was a better worke
and more acceptable to God , then all*
                              the

the Holocausts and other Sacrifices of the Lawe . Then our Lord liking the speech of this man, did praise him saying; *Thou art not farre from the kingdome of God* . Which is as much as to say ; Thou art not farre from beleeuing, and obeying the Ghospell, and obteining true saluation . For the knowing of a diuine truth so important, and the approouing it by the supernaturall gift of God , was a disposition for the being conuerted to him : and to acknowledge *Christ* himselfe, who was sent into the world to saue it.

Christ our Lord , if he would haue encreased his Iustice, vpon these two learned mē in the Law, might haue seuerely reprooued the ill mind, wherewith they were come to him; and he might haue discouered the craft , and malice, which they carryed in their hearts;

hearts ; for fo alfo they would
haue vnderftood , that he knew
all things, and thereby he might
haue put them to confufion and
fhame.Yet this he would not do;
but he heard them with admirable meekenes,and anfwered their
queftions with fupreme *Charity.*
And he approoued that which
they had faid well,though it were
very little , and very imperfect;
and he praifed it with ftrange *Benignity:*that fo he might remooue
that peruerfenes of minde from
thē, which they brought to him;
and encourage them to encreafe
in the knowledge and loue of
truth, till at length, they might
grow fubiect to it. And fo by this
true *Benignity*, he changed their
hearts , and fent them bettered
from him;and he taught vs withall,that not only we are to praife
good men, for the true vertue
which

which they haue, but that we may
alſo praiſe with moderation, euen
in imperfect and wicked men, the
good they doe or ſay; to the end
that they may growe to take affection to vertue, and may ſo deteſt and driue out of their hearts,
the wickednes which they haue,
and goe encreaſing in the good
way begunne; as alſo to gaine
their good will; & to make them
beneuolous and kinde; which is
a very good diſpoſition, towards
the inducing them to receiue in
good part the doctrine, which we
ſhall deliuer, and the reprehenſions, which we may haue cauſe
to vſe. And therefore Saint *Gre-*
gory aduiſeth, that when they who
are endowed with authority, and
wiſdome for this purpoſe, reproue ſinners, who are puſillanimous & weak, they ſhal do wel to
mingle ſome ſweetnes of praiſe,
                              with

the sharpenes of correction; that
so they may the better admit of
the doctrine and reproofe, which
is giuen them. The Saint expres-
seth it in these words. Wee shall
better drawe such sinners , as are
not peruerse & proud, but weake
and poore of heart , to the way
of heauen,if whilst we reprehend
the euil thinges, which they haue
done , wee ioyntly praise those
good thinges , which wee know
to be in them;to the end that by
this meanes,such praise may confirme and strengthen the in their
weakenes, who were humbled by
that reproofe . Thus did S. *Paule*
proceed with those Christians of
Thessalonica. For they, hauing fallen into the fault of giuing credit to certaine false Prophets who
taught the that the day of iudgment was then to come very sud-
denly , (whereby they were put
                K   into

into much diforder and trouble)
before he reprehended this light-
nes of theirs, he praifed them faying, 2. *Theff*. 1. *Wee muft giue many*
thanks to God, for the great encreafe
of yours faith, which is growing euery
day; and for the encreafe alfo of your
fraternall charity, which aboundeth in
euery one of you; and encreafeth daily,
both by your louing, and doing good to
one another. But when he had praifed them in thefe & other words,
he benignely reprehendeth them
faying, *chap*. 2. Wee befeech you
brethren, by the coming of *Chrift*
our Lord to iudgment, and by
the glorious and blefled vnion
which wee are all to haue together at that day, that you depart
not fo eafily from giuing credit
to vs; and from hauing the true
fence of thofe thinges which you
haue learned of vs; and that you
be not troubled, or frighted by
what

what others tell you ; and in a
word that none may haue power
to deceiue you; By this diuine ar-
tifice, the sacred *Doctour of the na-*
tions, did reprehend them ; when
first he had comforted and encouraged thē by recording that vertue, which he knew to be in them,
and the good opinion which he
had of them; to the end that, hauing cōpunction to, see that they
had failed of the good which they
had begunne , they might the
better accept of the reproofe he
gaue them; and so might reforme
themselues thereby.

K 2   THE

THE XIX. CHAPTER.

How wee must praise vertue, for the making it be more esteemed : and of the examples which Christ our Lord gaue vs to this purpose.

WEe must also praise the vertue of good men, to declare how great a good that is; and how that which seemeth little and of meane value in the sight of mé, is indeed very great, and hath a most high reward in the sight of God; to the end that other men may esteem greatly of it, and carry much affection to it, & labour hard to acquire it. Let vs deliuer some examples hereof.

Saint *Peter Matt.* 16. confessed to *Christ* our Lord that he was the true Sonne of God saying; *Thou art Christ the Sonne of the liuing God.*

It

It seemed a small matter, and of
no merit, that Saint *Peter*, hauing
conuerfed fo long with *Chrift* our
Lord, & feen with his owne eyes,
fo great and fo euident miracles,
and heard fuch doctrine, & con-
templated fuch an exáple of life;
that he fhould pioufly incline his
heart to belieue, that he was the
true *Meſſias*, & the naturall Sonne
of God. For this did not coft him
the fhedding of his blood, nor
the tormenting of his body with
affliction, and penance; but only
to produce a pious affect of the
will, and to performe an act of
obedience in the vnderftanding.
But *Chrift* our Lord praifed him,
and gaue teftimony that this inward act of his was of fupreme
value and eftimation, in the
fight of Almighty God, and that
on earth he fhould receiue admirable fauours from God for the
K 3   fame;

fame;&that in heauen,he fhould enioy an imméfe reward of glory. And that frō that inflāt,he might begin to be happy by that certen hope, and pawne, which was giuen him of that infinite good, which he was afterward to poffeffe , and enioy during all eternity . All this he declared by faying ; *Bleffed art thou Simon the fonne of Ionas.* for men who are made of flefh and blood , were not able, with al the humane wifdome they haue,to teach thee this truth. My celeftiall Father it is , who hath reueiled it to thee, & vpon thee, will I build my Church , and to thee will I giue the keyes of the kingdome of heauen.

By thefe words, *Chrift* our Lord praifed by faith and deuotion of Saint *Peter*; and declared to the world , of how foueraigne value before Almighty God , and how
richly

richly to be rewarded with celeftiall and eternall bleffings , one
fingle act of vertue may be,which
is performed by a iuft mã,though
it be eafily produced , and in a
fhort time, and how little foeuer
it may coft; and efpecially an interiour act of liuely faith, which
a iuft man hath no difficulty at
all to performe.

Chrift our Lord , being in the
Atrium of the Temple *Matc.* 12.
Luc. 21. behoulding thé who were
cafting almes into the cheft ,
which was to ferue for the repa-
ration of the Temple , for the
maintenance of the Priefts , and
for the relief of the poore; amõgſt
the reft of them who caſt in their
almes , which without doubt was
then done both by many and in
plentifull manner(for it was neer
Eafter, at which time there came
much people to *Ierufalem* , from

all parts ;) there cometh a very
poore widow, and casteth into the
chest, two of the least little peeces
of money or mites. Our Lord
seeing her and being pleased to
praise her much, for the act which
shee had done, and the almes
which shee had giuen, called his
disciples, and pointing out the
woman said thus to them. *This*
widow hath cast a greater almes into
the chest, and made a greater present to the Temple, *then all the*
rest, *who haue giuen almes this day.*
And our Lord shewed diuers reasons, why shee had giuen more
then any of them. Firtt, becaufe
in proportion of her poore condition, it was more for her to giue
a mite, then for others to giue
store of crownes. And becaufe the
rest gaue the almes out of that
which did aduance beyond their
necessary maintenance; and that
they

they gaue not all,but a parr therof; but this widow gaue that
which was neceſſary ro her ſelfe,
and ſhee gaue it all. But the principall reaſon which he was pleaſed to ſignify vnder this was, for
that ſhee gaue her almes, with a
greater affection and deſire to
giue, and with more ardour of
charity then al they;which he declared by her hauing giuen all
that ſhe had,being in preciſe neceſſity thereof, for her owne re-
liefe.

In this ſorte did *Chriſt* our Lord
praiſe the almes of this poore widow, and by praiſing her,he ma-
nifeſted to all the children of his
Church, how highly the good
worke of a iuſt perſon is valued,
in the ſight of Almighty God; &
the great account he makes therof, and how he will reward it in
heauen; and how he meanes not

K 5   to

to giue the reward according to
the quantity of the worke, but
according to the good will and
loue of God and our neighbour,
wherewith it is performed . He
will alfo haue vs learne frō hence,
firſt to esteem greatly of the good
works, which our neighbours do,
how litle soeuer they may be; and
and approue them and praiſe thē,
before men, for their edification;
and much to value thoſe good
men, who doe them, though they
be poore; & of meane condition
and eſtate; ſince God; who ſees
their hearts , doth prize them
much. And ſecondly, he will haue
vs learne by this, to be animated
towards the doing of good works,
and to exerciſe the acts of Religion and charity, with much affection , and deſire to pleaſe God;
and to doe more then wee doe; although by reaſon of our weaknes,
                              and

and our little talent, either of
vertue, or goods, or power any
other way, our workes be very
fmall; fince God hath regard to
the good will, wherewith they are
done, & to the pious heart, from
whence they proceed.

The Apoftle Saint *Paule* followed this example of *Chrift* our
Lord. Who (to animate the *Corinthians*, to giue almes to the Chriftians, who were in want at *Ierufalem*; and that none of thé fhould
omit to giue according to his
power, how little foeuer that
might be) did praife the vertue
and charity, which they of *Macedonia* had fhewed to the fame
Chriftians, affifting them liberally with almes, according to
the power of euery one. And he
praifeth them in thefe wordes, *2.
Cor. 8. Wee giue you brethren to vnderftand*, the gratious, and liberall
K 6   gift

gift which God communicated
by his goodnes, to the Churches
of *Macedonia*, who receauing many
grieuous persecutions from the
Gentiles, (who afflicted, and affronted, and robbed them of the
goods they had) did yet abound
with ioy in their very tribula-
tions, and they did not onely accept of them with patience, but
with interiour ioy, yea and that
a very great ioy, for the loue of
Christ our Lord, for whom they
suffered, and through the hope of
celestiall blessings, which God
promiseth to them who suffer for
the loue of him. And being poore
they were all, according to their
weake power and strength, so liberall in giuing, that they did
very abundatly discouer the pure
intention which they had therin,
and their great promptitude, and
euen hunger and thirst to giue,

and

& to pleaſe God by doing all tho
good, that poſſibly they could, to
their neighbours. And I giue teſtimony to this truth, that not
only they gaue willingly all they
could, but more then they could;
for not onely gaue they of tho
ſuperfluity, and that which they
could conueniétly ſpare, but they
gaue part of thoſe very thinges,
which were euen neceſſary for the
very ſupport of their liues.

The Apoſtle, hauing praiſed
in theſe wordes, the Charity and
mercy of the *Macedonians*, inui-
teth the *Corinthians* by the induce-
ment of this example, to doe
the like; and he ſaith, that conſidering what the Chriſtians of
Macedonia haue done, I haue perſwaded my ſelf to ſed *Titus* to you,
that this grace which he begun
in you, may be finiſhed and per-
fected by his exhorting, & moouing

uing you to giue almes to the
Chriftians who fuffer in *Ierufalem*;
and by procuring , that all men
may giue what they can; & that
it may be put all together , and
fent to *Ierufalem* , as was done by
thē of *Macedonia* . And he wifheth
them moreouer , that euen they,
who haue but little to giue ,
fhould yet giue fome what euen
of that little, with a ready minde,
and a defirous good will,to giue
more if they could. And he affirmeth, and teftifieth , on the part
of God,that the litle,which they
fhould giue with fuch affe&ion
& good will,would greatly pleafe
God , and be much efteemed by
him;and be alfo rewarded according to the goodwill wherewith
they gaue.For he faith,if the will
be ready and efficacioufly prepa-
red to doe good, it is very acceptable and pleafing to God,if they
                              worke

worke & giue according to what
they haue, or can performe; and
God doth not require, for the
making men acceptable to him,
that they fhould giue or do, what
they cannot giue or do.

THE XX. CHAPTER.

How it is fit to praife the vertue of
fome, thereby to correct the vice
of others.

ANother way, which makes
our praifing others to be
very profitable for vs, and pleafing to almighty God, is to praife
the vertue, and good workes of
them, from whom no fuch thing
had been expected; and thereby
to conuince and confound thofe
others, who were not fo vertuous,
and did not worke fo well, not-
withftanding that they had greater helpes, and were in greater
obli-

obligations then the former. Let
vs declare this by an example.

There was a *Centurion* (that is to
fay a Captaine of a hundred foul-
diers) in *Capharnaum, Matt.* 8. *Luc,*
7. placed there by the Romans;
and a Gentile he was, who defcended not from Patriarches, & Prophets, but from Gentiles & Ido-
laters, and from people who had
noe knowledge of the true God.
This man, by meanes of conuerfation, which he had with the
Iewes, came to know this truth,
that there was one God; and he
had taken an affection to his holy
Lawe, and to his people of *Ifraell;*
and he loued & cherifhed them,
and built a Sinagogue for them,
vpon the vnderftanding which
he had, that of all the men in the
world, thefe were the profeffors
of true Religion. This *Centurion,*
had a feruant whom he greatly
loued,

Ioued, who fell ficke of a pleurify,
& was growne to the very point
of death . And the feruant being
in thofe termes , and the Mafter
hauing heard of the miracles
which had been wrought by *Chrift*
our Lord , he conceiued a great
confidence and faith , that if he
defired remedy for that feruant,
he fhould obtaine it ; and he belieued with great affurednes, that
Chrift was a Lord fo powerfull,
that euen in abfence, he could
giue him the life , and health of
his feruant , by the onely com-
maüdment of his word. Not pre-
fuming therfore to appeare in the
prefence of *Chrift* our Lord , (as
holding himfelfe vnworthy therof) he interpofed the auncient,
and prime men of the Iewes, for
interceffours . Thefe men therfore , in the name of the *Centurion,* defired that he would goe to
his

his houfe , and cure his feruant:
inftantly our Lord put himfelfe
vpon the way, to doe as much as
they defired. As foon as the *Centurion* knew that *Chrift* our Lord
was comminge to his houfe , he
tould him, by meanes of the fame
interceffours , that in no cafe he
was to doe it ; for that himfelfe
was vnworthy of fo great honour, but he onely prayed , that
from thence, he would commaũd
by fome one word of his, that his
feruant might be cured; and that
that would ferue for his recouery.
And this he confirmed by the example of his owne perfon; for if
he, being a weake man, and fubiect to the commaũd of another,
(who was the Generall of the Army) could yet commaund his fol-
diers, to difpofe themfelues here
or there , and that accordingly,
and inftantly the thing was done;
                  how

how much more could *Christ* our
Lord, being so absolute, and of
so great power, commaund from
wherefoeuer he were, that sicknes
and death should be gone, and
that health and life should come;
and that they would not faile to
obey him.

This man, discouered great humility in not presuming once to
to appeare in the presence of
Christ our Lord, but to negotiate
by meanes of the Iewes, whom he
held for better then himselfe; and
by those wordes, he also shewed a
great faith . And so *Christ* our
Lord, hauing heard this message,
shewed to be in admiration, to see
so great faith in a Pagan soul-
dier. And turning his countenáce
to the troupe of Iewes, who followed him, he said ; *Verily I say to
you, I haue not found so great faith as
this, in Israell. And many shall come
from*

from the East, and from the West, *and from all the parts of the* world , *out of the nations of the Gentiles* , and by meanes of faith;and obedience to my Ghofpell , *shall sit in company of Abraham, Isaac , and Iacob* , and the reft of the Patriarches ; and fhall raigne with God: *and* on the other fide, they who be *the children of the kingdom,* which are the Iewes, who defced from the Patriarchs, and to whom the promife of the *Mefsias* and of his celeftiall king-dome was made , *shall* the moft part of them *be excluded from that Kingdome , and shut vp into eternall torment.*

Chrift our Lord praifed the faith of the *Centurion,* for the reproofe of the infidelity of thofe Iewes, who belieued not in him at all; & of the weak faith of fome others, who belieued in him; and to con-found them by this example;and

to

to mooue them to penance for
their fault, and to perſwade with
them, who belieued not ; and to
encreaſe their faith who beleeued. And ſo he was pleaſed to expreſſe himſelfe to this effect; This
Centurion being a Gentile , and
not hauing read the Prophets,
nor hauing been brought vp in
the Lawe of God, nor in any diſ-
cipline, but of the warre, and not
hauing ſeene my workes and miracles , but onely heard relation
of mee; hath beleeued my truth,
and my power, with ſo great and
ſo firme a faith; and on the other
ſide , the children of *Iſraell*, who
are deſcended from the Patriarches, & who haue read the Scriptures , and know the Prophecies,
which ſpeake of mee ; and who
were looking for mee, and haue
ſeen my miracles , and heard my
doctrine, ſome of theſe, haue not
beliе-

belieued in mee, nor will receiue
my truth, but perſecute the ſame;
& others haue beleeued it ſo im-
perfectly, that none of them hath
arriued to ſo great a Faith as this
man hath, and as he confeſſeth in
honour of mee. They I ſay, notwithſtanding the many cauſes &
motiues, which they haue had, to
beleeue my truth with a perfect
faith, haue not beleeued it, as
they ought: and this man hauing
had ſo few motiues, as he had to
beleeue in me, hath beleeued with
ſo great perfection, that he hath
farre outſtripped all thereſt. And
therefore this man, though but a
Gentile; and all the other Gentiles alſo, who throughout all the
parts of the world, ſhall be conuerted to mee, and ſhall be like
this man in his faith, and obedience to my word, ſhall be ad-
mitted into the Kingdom of heauen,

uen, in company of the holy Patriarches, whom they haue imitated; and on the other fide the
children of *Ifraell,*who according
to the extra&iō of flefh & blood,
defcend from Patriarches;if they
doe not penance, and reforme
their infidelity and difobedience,
by true and conftant faith, and
reall fubie&ion to my com-
maundments, fhall be excluded
from the Kingdome of heauen,
and condemned to eternall torments.

In this fort did *Chrift* our Lord
praife the faith of the *Centurion*;
and thereby did he corre& the infidelity,or at leaft the weake faith
of the Iewes. And he did it with
much reafon; for the faith of this
man was fo great, that fome of
the Saints conceiue, that he did
truly know,and beleeue the diuinity of *Chrift* our Lord; and that
it

it was couered with the veile of his facred humanity. For thus faith Saint *Hierome.* The wifdome of the *Centurion* is difcouered, in that with the eyes of faith, he faw the diuinity which lay hid vnder that veile of humanity. And the fame doth Saint *Auguftin* confeffe, faying, in the perfon of the fame *Centurion* ; If I, being a man fub-iect to others, haue yet power to commaund; how much more haft thou it, ô Lord, whom all the powers of the earth obey and ferue?

Wee are to profit by this ex-ample of *Chrift* our Lord, in prai-fing fuch feruants of God, as liue in a more eminent degree of ver-tue, then the ftate and condition of their life feemeth to exact at their hands; for the admonifhing and correcting of others, who, by reafon of their vocation, and of
　　　　　　　　　　the

the parts and gifts which God
hath beftowed vpon them, were
obliged to greater vertue. As
when, for the correcting of fome
Prelate, who may be ftraight handed in giuing almes, and negli-
gent withall, in the gouernment
of his fubiects, we may praife
fome Lord, who being a fecular
man, is yet moft liberall in giuing almes, and moft vigilant in
procuring that his feruants and
vaffailes may be vertuous. And as
if, for the reproofe and amendment of a Religious man, who
were remiffe in making Prayer,
and doing Penance, and were full
of tepidity in the exercife of vertue, and imperfect in the performance of his *Obedience*, we fhould
praife a fecular Cauallier, for
being much giuen to prayer, and
diligent in the mortification of
himfelfe, and full of feruour in

L   the

the exercise of vertue, and very
obedient to his Ghoftly Father.
For we frame the reafon after this
manner; If a Lord or a Cauallier, being a fecular man, be of
fo great recollection, fo great
vertue, fuch purity of life, fuch
diligence in the doing of good
workes, his vocation not feeming
to bind him altogether to it;how
much more reafon is it, that a
Prelate make himfelfe a poffeffor
of thefe vertues, whom his ftate
obligeth to be a perfect man;and
a Religious perfon,whom his Religion obligeth to procure to be
perfectly vertuous?

And fo to reforme fome very
wife and learned man, who wanteth fpirit and deuotion, we may
praife a man who is wholly ignorant, but yet full of the fpirit of
God, and of true deuotion faying: If this rude creature hauing

so little knowledge of God, and
of his workes, and mysteries, and
being able to vse so little difcourfe of reafon, haue yet so
great loue of God, and fo great
feeling of his goodnes, and of his
mysteries, and workes, & fo great
guft of diuine things, and maketh
so great eftimation of vertue, and
fpirituall bleffings; how much
more is it reafon, that a wife and
learned man, to whom God hath
giuen fo great wit, & knowledge,
for the comprehending of truth
both diuine and humane, and fo
great light of reafo to difcourfe,
and paffe by meanes of vifible
thinges to the knowledge of fuch
as are inuifible, and by the creatures, to come to the knowledge
and loue of the Creatour, haue
fuch deuotion, as was faid before,
or at leaft procure to haue it?

In this fort did the Apoftle S.

Paule, following this example of
Chrift our Lord, cōmend the Gentiles who were conuerted, for the
moft excellēt vertues which they
had , and the admirable workes
they did, and for thofe moft high
gifts, which God had communicated to them, by meanes of their
faith; to the end that fo the Iewes,
who were in their infidelity ,
might know their errour, and be
in confufion, for their wickednes;
and might be awaked by the vertue of the Gentiles , and encouraged to the incitation thereof.
This did he fignify by faying,
Rom. 11. *For as much as I am an Apoftle of the Gentiles,* and during the
whole time that I fhall be fo , *I
will honour this miniftery,* taking
paines , and fuffering for them,
to bring them to the faith who
are not yet come to it , and to
confirme and perfect them with
vertues,

vertues, and the gifts of God who haue already receiued it. And by this meanes, I will procure the conuersion of the Iewes, who are of my kinred according to the flesh, to the end that they, behoulding the most abūdant fruite which is produced in the Gentiles, and the most pretious gifts which God cōmunicated to them by meanes of their faith, *may be moued to a holy emulation, and imitation of them, and so some of them may be saued.*

THE XXI. CHAPTER.

How wee are to praise the vertue of our neighbours, to defend them so, from some vniust slaunder.

ANother very iust reason, for which wee must praise our neighbours, and commend their

vertues, and good workes, is to
defend them from some slaunder,
or false testimony, or some detraction or affront, wherewith their
reputation is vniustly spotted, &
their good name and the opinion
of their vertue obscured . Let vs
deliuer an example, which *Christ*
our Lord left vs of this truth.

Christ our Lord being in *Bethania*, at supper in the house of *Simon*
the leaper, *Ioh.* 12. *Matth.* 26. *Mary
Magdalen* came with an Alablaster
box, full of very odoriferous and
pretious ointment, & she anointed the feet of our Lord with it,
& filled the whole house with the
sweet odour. Now *Iudas* began to
murmur at this worke , and to
speake ill of the holy woman , in
that she had wasted the ointmet,
which was of so great value, that
it might haue beé sould for three
hundred peeces of money , and
been

been giuen to the poore. And the
reft of the difciples, feeing the indignation and murmuringe of
Iudas, and not vnderftanding the
root of malice , from whence it
grew, like good fimple men conceiued that he had reafon , for
what he faid ; and were induced
by his example, to murmur too,
and to reproue that good worke,
which *Mary* with fo great deuotion, had done.

Now our Lord faw well how
the difciples murmured againft
this holy woman, without all reafon; efteeming that to be vitious,
which was an act of vertue, and
fpeaking ill of that , which was
well done . For being a cuftome
of the coûtry, as it was, to anoint
the feet of their guefts, with pretious ointméts, if they were eminent men; it was no euill , but a
good worke to doe that , which

was in vſe for ſome good and ho-
neſt end. For an indifferent actiō,
ſuch an one as this was, is made
good by addreſſing it to a vertuous end. But then to this is to
be added, the pure intention, and
great deuotion, wherewith *Mary*
did this worke: for ſhe did it as
being moued by piety and religion, to exhibite honour and veneration to our Lord, whom ſhe
knew to be worthy of all poſſible
reuerence and reſpect.

Our Lord therefore on the one
ſide ſeeing the goodnes of the
worke & conſidering moreouer,
the myſtery which himſelf mēt to
ſignify thereby, who had moued
her to it; and on the other obſeruing the raſh iudgment & murmuring of the diſciples, and eſpecially of *Iudas*, who was the
ſpring of all that ill, he began to
defend the woman, and to praiſe
the

the good worke which fhe had
wrought , and to difcharge the
flaunder , whereby they thought
to doe her wrong ; faying after
this manner; W *by are you trouble-*
fome to this woman ? Why are you
enraged againft her? Why thinke
and fpeake you ill of her worke?
leaue her free frō your reproach,
and giue her leaue to keep this
ointment , for my buriall . His
meaning was to fay , the bodies
of dead men , are according to
our cuftome , to be anointed before they be interred ; and this
woman would be glad to anoint
my body, when I fhall be dead; &
then will not be able, becaufe that
office will be firft performed by
others , before I be buried ; and
after that buriall, fhe fhal be preuented by my refurrection . But
fuffer her to doe that now, which
fhe would doe them; and that fhe

may signify by this vnction that
I am to dy; and that my body will
be soon laid in the graue, and she
in the meane time, doth but performe that office of piety, which
is performed to other dead bodies.

Our Lord said further, *she hath*
wrought a good worke towards mee;
and it was conuenient that shee
should doe it, although by doing
it, the price of this ointment were
thereby not giuen to the poore.
For the poore you shall haue allwaies with you, and so shall you
euer haue oportunity, and occasion to doe good to them: but as
for mee, you shall not allwaies
haue me with you, in this visible
forme; for I am quickly to leaue
this world, and to goe to my Father. And I tell you for certaine,
that in whatsoeuer part of the
world, the good newes of this
Ghospell

Ghofpell fhall be preached, the
worke of this woman fhall be re-
counted, and celebrated in her
memory, and for her glory in all
the parts of the world. And by
thefe words did *Chrift* our Lord
defend the *Magdalena*, and praife
her good worke.

From this example we are firft
to fetch this fruite, to make great
eftimation of good workes, how
little, how light, and how eafy fo
euer they may be. How eafy a
thing is it, for a rich woman to
buy a pound of pretious ointmét,
for three húdred peeces of filuer,
and to anoint the feet of a holy
man therwith; efpecially of fuch
a Saint as *Chrift* our Lord was?
For in that he, who was anointed,
was fo great a Lord, the worke
became more fweet, and eafy to
be performed. Well then, fo light
and eafy a worke as this, for ha-

uing been performed by a perfon
who was in the ftate of grace, and
with a pure intention, to ferue
and pleafe Almighty God, was
efteemed fo highly, as wee fee by
Chrift our Lord, and praifed with
fuch Maiefty of wordes; and rewarded with fuch a high reward,
both in heauen and earth. Such
value and dignity and excellency
haue thofe good workes, which
are done for the loue of God.

If the *Magdalena* had fpent, not
thrée hundred peeces of filuer,
but three hundred thoufand, in
the feruice of the world, as in bra-
ueries, and vaine dreffings, in curious and delitious bankets, and
in making fome feaft, & triumph
to giue delight and guft, as louers
of the world are wont to doe; all
that expence, had been loft, and
fhe had not pleafed Almighty
God therby; nor had merited any
thing

thing is his fight; and there had
been no honorable memory therof continued amongſt men. And
not reaping any profit by them,
ſhee would haue incurred many
faultes, as ordinarily there are, in
theſe thinges, which would haue
condemned her, either to the re-
porary paines of Purgatory, or
els to the eternall torments of
hell. But now, for hauing ſpent
a little money vpon the ſeruice
of *Chriſt* our Lord, and for vnder-
going that light & ſweet labour,
in performing that work of piety,
with her owne hands, ſhe pleaſed
Almighty God ſo much, and merited ſo greatly in his fight, & obtained ſo much honour throughout the world, that as long as it
laſts, ſhe ſhall be praiſed, & had
in veneration for this worke, by
all faithfull Chriſtians; and for
all eternity ſhall be made happy
amongſt

amongſt the Angells in heauen, with a moſt high crown of glory. And ſo will that be fulfilled which was ſaid by the wiſe man; *The memory of iuſt perſons wil remaine amõgſt men, after their death,* and they ſhall relate their heroicall deedes, and exhibite praiſe, and veneration to them; whereas the memory and fame of wicked perſons, ſhall be full of reproach, and it ſhall periſh.

Secondly, we are to draw from this example of *Chriſt* our Lord, that when wee ſee vertuous people ſuffer hurt in their reputatiõ, or good name, whereby their neighbours were to be edified, & whereof they are depriued by the ſlaunders, and lies of wicked people, wee muſt defend them by giuing teſtimony to the truth, and by praiſing their good life. And when men murmur againſt them

in

in our prefence, wee muft excufe
their innocency, & declare their
vertue. And if it fo fall out, that
we haue any credit with the mur-
murers,we muft procure to mend
them,and ftop the difcourfe; and
if our aduice by way of fpeech
will not ferue,we muft fhew both
by our filence, and by our countenance, that fuch murmuring is
difpleafing to vs . This is that
which the holy Ghoft doth ad-
monifh faying,that as the fharpe
cold winde coming from the
North, hindreth raine, and per-
mits not, through the coldnes
thereof, that the cloudes fhould
eafily diffolue thefelues into water; fo doth the referued and fad
countenáce,of him who heareth,
ty vp the tongue of the murmurer . This faith the W*ife man* in
the *Prouerbs*, who was inftructed
by the Holy Ghoft, And the reafon

fon is, becaufe when the murmurer fees, that they who heare him
looke cheerfully vpon the matter, he thinkes he pleafeth them,
& that they giue him a glad eare;
and he taketh fo much the more
heart, and liberty to murmur: but
whé he findeth, that they fhew him
an ill countenance, he vnderftáds
by that, that the difcourfe pleafeth nor; but that they are vnwil-
ling to heare it, & this he markes,
and fo he begines to giue ouer
murmuring.

THE XXII. CHAPTER.

How wee ought to praife wife men,
when they are vertuous, to the end
that others may profit by their ex-
ample and doctrine.

BEfides thofe reafons before
expreffed, there is yet an
other,

other of great force , why wee
ought to praise the seruants of
God;and it is,to the end that our
neighbours hauing notice of
their vertue and parts,may profit more, both by their doctrine,
and by the example of their life.
This praise belongeth chiefly, to
persons who are much knowne,
and haue authority, or publicke
office, as Prelates, Iudges, Preachers,Cófessors, Religious men,
Priests , and rich and noble persons;for vpon the vertue, & prudence , and wisdome of such as
these (who are as the heads , and
hearts) dependeth the vertue of
the people: and so the good life,
and incorrupt doctrine of these
seruants of God, being generally
knowne , and commended , the
rest of men doth profit by it so
much the more,and are more edified by their good speeches, and
ver-

vertuous examples; and therfore
to praise such persons, with that
discretion which is fit, is a thing
very acceptable to God, and
very profitable for the gaining of
soules. Let vs relate an example,
which *Chrift* our Lord gaue vs
hereof.

The disciples of Saint *Iohn Bap-*
tift, came to *Chrift* our Lord in
their Masters name, *Mat. 11. Luc. 7.*
to know if he were that *Chrift*, who
was to come; that is to say, if he
were the *Mefsias*, who had been
promised by Almighty God, for
the saluation of the world. And
our Lord hauing answered this
question, by the workes he did,
which was by working the miracles which were prophecied of the
Mefsias, and by preaching that doctrine which belonged to him to
teach, and publish, he dispatched
them away saying; *Tell Iohn what*
you

you haue seen and heard . When the
disciples of Saint *Iohn* were gone,
our Lord began to celebrate the
diuine praises of the same Saint
Iohn, and to proclame his admirable vertues, saying; *What went
you out to see in the desert? Went you
perhaps to see some reed, or cane, which
is shaken with euery winde? or some
man set forth in soft, and delicate ap-
parell?* He meat as followeth; you
went not out to see a light, or vn-
constant person, who is mooued
by euery passion, or interest; but
a most constant man, and who
perseuereth with admirable reso-
lution, in the truth, which he
preacheth; and in that holy life
which he began to lead. And you
shall euidently see, that incon-
stant and light persons, who are
mooued with passions, or by the
interests of this world, be allwaies
in loue with regaloes, and delica-
cies

cies in their food, their cloathing, and their habitation, and
are desirous of wealth, and haue
recourse to the houses of great
men, where these things are foūd
in abundance. But in *Iohn*, you
shall see nothing of this, but a life
of great penance and austerity, &
very abstinent, & estranged from
all manner of regalo, and wholly
depriued & destitute of all earthly goods. For his habitation, is
in the dry and horrid desert: his
bed, is the hard ground: his garment is a sharpe haire cloth, made
of camells haire: his food is dry
locusts: his drinke running water;
and his continuall exercise, is to
pray, and contemplate in that desert, and to baptise and preach
penance, in the riuer of *Iordan.*
He saith moreouer of him; *And
what went you out to see in the desert?
Was it perhaps some Prophet? Verely
I say*

I *fay to you, that he is more then a Pro-*
phet. For this is he, of whom the eter-
nall Father faid, whileft he was fpeak-
ing to his fonne, as is recorded in Ma-
lachias; *Behould I fend my Angell be-*
fore thy prefence, to prepare the way
for thee. I *tell you for a moft certaine*
truth, that there was not borne of woe-
men a greater, then Iohn the Baptift;
but yet he, who is the leaft in the king-
dome of heauen is greater then hee.
Which fignifieth , according to
the beft expofition ; He who for
his age, & the office of humility
which he exercifeth , and in opinion of the people is the pooreft
member of the Church , (which
was our Lord himfelfe the true
Meffias) is both in dignity , and
fanctity, grea er then he.

Saint *Iohn* had preached penance to the people , and exhorted men to the exercife of all vertue, and had giuen expreffe teftimony

mony of *Chrift* our Lord , affirming that he was the *Mefsias*. And
now, to the end, that by fending
this meffage, whereby they asked
of *Chrift* our Lord , *if he were the
Mefsias* , the people might not
fufpect that he made any doubt,
as fome inconftant might doe, of
that which formerly he had teftified , and of that which now he
queftioned , but only in regard
both of his owne difciples, and of
al that people (that fo they might
forfake the ignorance, wherein
they were, & remain more confirmed in their faith ; & not thinke
that he demaunded it in regard
of the ignorance wherein himfelf was) for this reafon, did *Chrift*
our Lord extoll him afterward,
with fo illuftrious praifes , and
teftified with fo great affeueratiõ,
the conftancy and purity of his
life, and the eminency of his per-
                                    fon

son and diguity. And he proued
this , both by the experience of
what they sawe, and by the testimony also of a Prophet : to the
end that they might be settled in
the great belief, which they ought
to haue of his truth, and sanctity;
and that so, they might profit by
the doctrine, which he had preached , and the example of life
which he had shewed.

In this sort are wee to praise
men for their vertues , after the
example of *Chrift* our Lord : because their life and doctrine concerne the good of the faithfull,
to the end that their wordes of
counsell, may be more effica-
cious , and their example more
profitable to all men . Thus did
Saint *Paule* proceed; who, resol-
uing to send *Timothy* a most faithfull instrument of the Ghospell,
to preach and administer holy
thinges,

thinges, at *Philippos* a Citty of *Macedonia*, doth praise him first in a letter, which he writeth to the *Philippians*, wherin he teſtifieth his vertues, ſaying, *I hope in the mercy of Chriſt our Lord that I shall very shortly be able to ſend Timothy to you.* And *I haue deſigned to ſend him in particular, becauſe I haue none other, who is ſo agreeable to mee, and ſo of one heart with my ſelfe, and who with ſo pure loue and true charity, hath ſo particular a care of your good.*

These and other praiſes, did S. *Paule* deliuer of *Timothy*; to the end that the *Philippians*, might receiue him with great eſtimation of his ſanctity, and zeale, and might profit by him. And he did the like, when he reſolued to ſend *Titus* a ſeruant of *Chriſt* our Lord, and a preacher of the Ghoſpell to them of *Corinthus*: for firſt he praiſed him, ſaying to this effect; *I*

giue

giue great thankes to God, for *inspiring* the heart of *Titus* with the same desire, that I haue, and for hauing kindled him with the same loue and endewed him with the same desire of your spirituall profit, which he gaue to mee. With these & other wordes, Saint *Paule* praised *Titus*, to the end that his labours might prooue of greater spirituall profit to the *Corinthians*. And after this manner, are we also to praise Prelats, Preachers, Gouernours of Citties, Paftours of foules, Religious men, and Priefts, and all fuch as haue publicke office, and authority ouer the people, when they clearly expreffe true vertue in their liues. For. when they are knowne for fuch, and that they are wife, and diligent in doing their duties, they fhall profit the people more, and efpecially fuch families thereof, as conuerfe with

M them.

them *Let vs praise* (faith *Ecclesia-*
ſticus) *ſuch men as are excellently glo-*
rious, aboue the reſt.

THE XXIII. CHAPTER.

Of the rule which wee are to hold,
when vpon the aforeſaid reaſon,
we ſhall praiſe the ſeruants
of God.

BVt in affoarding this praiſe,
wee muſt obſerue theſe directions, and rules of diſcretion.
That whē we praiſe another man,
not to the end of encouraging
him, or moouing him to the pra-
ctiſe and proceeding in vertue,
or for the perſwading him to the
doing of ſome good worke, but
for the good, and profit of others,
that ſo his vertue and wiſdome
being knowne, and much eſtee-
med, his neighbours, who heare,
and

and difcourfe thereof, may profit
by his example, inftruction, aduice and gouernment (which is
the cafe wherof we are fpeaking;)
we muft not then praife the party
in his own prefece, nor yet before
his familiar friends, who already
know his parts, and who are likely
to tell him what they haue heard;
but onely before fuch others, whō
it may concerne to know his vertues and parts, to take profit by
him. So did *Chrift* our Lord, whē
he praifed Saint *Iohn* ; for he did
it in his abfence; and he ftaied for
the doing of it, till the difciples
of Saint *Iohn* were gone.

This rule muft wee alfo hold,
that fo we may take from the feruant of God, whom we praife, all
occafion of vaine complacence,
and eftimation of himfelfe, efpecially when the praifes happen to
be great, in refpect that the par-

ties vertues, and parts are greatly
worthy to be praised . For although it be true, that many feruants of God , who haue laid the
rootes of humility very deeply in
their hearts, and who, by long
experience and much light from
heauen, haue wel vnderstood and
penetrated the weakenes of man,
are free from this danger, & take
no occasion of vanity by it , but
contemne themselues so much
the more ; yet this, is not euery
bodies case. Howsoeuer we see indeed, that it happened in the case
of Saint *Ambrose,* when once a diuell (speaking by the mouth of a
possest person) had a minde to
moue him to pride, and began to
cry out thus aloud , *Ambrose tor-*
ments mee; For then the Saint vnderstood the diuells craft, & what
he pretended by praising him .
But he did not onely not growe
                                     proud

proud by occasion thereof, but he
humiliated himselfe so much the
more , and said; *Hold thy peace,*
thou diuell, for it is not Ambrose who
torments thee, but the faith of the
Saints in God, and thine owne enuy.
Know that Ambrose will not growe
proud, vpon thy praises. This passed
with Saint *Ambrose*, and the like
happened to Saint *Marcellus*, the
Abbot. For this man , had a gift
from God, to cast out diuells; and
they brought diuers possest persons to him; and the diuells desiring, by their infernall craft , to
hoise vp the Saint, into pride with
praise, they cried out thus aloud,
Marcellus, doe thou commaund vs to de-
part out of these bodies , for thou hast
power ouer vs; and this they repea-
peated often . The Saint vnderstood the malice of the diuells,
& would not send them out vpon
their commaundmēt; but taking

occasion from that speech, to
humble him selfe so much the
more, and lifting vp his eyes to
heauen, he begged of *Christ* our
Lord, that he would cast them out
saying thus; *O Lord, preserue this
worke of thy hands*; & he continued
praying so long, that the diuells
departed out of the bodies.

Though this be so, and that
many great seruants of God, are
settled so firmely, and solidly in
the truth of humility, that humane praises moue them not at
all, but rather they humiliate
themselues the more by occasion
thereof; yet there are others, who
though indeed they be the seruát
of God and haue very excellent
vertues, and gifts from heauen,
and are worthy to be praised; yet
notwithstanding they haue some
weaknes this way, and are subiect
to the danger of growing proud
vpon

vpon humane praife , and efpecially whē they are praifed much.
And this is the vfuall cafe , and
which ordinarily happeneth,that
euen good men are fubiect to this
weaknes, and are expofed to this
danger . And a man may clearly
fee,what force thofe praifes haue
to make men giddy, & how much
occafion they minifter of making
them fall into vaine complacēce
and pride . Firft , in that the diuells , who are fo great and wife
Mafters in doing ill,did take the
meanes of praifing , and publi-
fhing the power which Saint *Am-
brofe*,and Saint *Marcellus* had ouer
them from Almighty God , as
the likelieft way to make them
fal into pride. And this truth may
bee alfo feene, by the great diligence,which the Saints haue euer
vfed , in flying from the praifes
of men, for the dāger which they

knew to be therein, and the feare
they had to fall thereby.

Surius doth relate in the life of
the bleſſed and moſt holy man
Iohn, who was a Prior of *Chanons
Regular*; that fearing the danger
of praiſe, he fled from it after an
extraordinary manner. He went
to do a certaine office of charity,
to certaine woemen the ſeruants
of God, who were retired from
the world; and one of them, who
was there ſhut vp, receaued a *Reuelation* of his going thither; and
therein, our Lord had declared
to them, the great ſanctity and
merit of that ſeruant of his. Now
there was here no neceſſity to recount that reuelation in praiſe of
his ſanctity: for it was not made
to her for the profit of the Saint,
but to the end that they might
profit by his coming thither, ſo
much the more, by how much
more

more they were certified of his
fanctity. And therefore , as soon
as the Saint heard her begin to
speake thereof, he found that
there was danger of conceiuing
some vaine complacence, or esti-
tion of himselfe; and it troubled
him much to heare such praises
of his vertue; and he made her a
quicke answere , and concluding
the busines in few wordes , went
imediatly away . For the danger
that he found , to heare humane
praise , made him resolue not to
stay , where there was so great
estimation of the holy manner of
his life.

Saint William, who of Duke of
Aquitania, came to be a most holy
Monke , and a Father of many
Monkes , was much praised by
men, for his many vertues, & the
great miracles which he wrought.
This put him to extreme paine,
M 5 and

and he would faine haue auoided the working of miracles, through the feare he had of being praifed. And *Theobaldus* the Bifhop , faith in his life; That in regard he was not able to edure humane praife, he went into a folitary place, & and betooke himfelfe there to a little cottage in company of a difciple of his , doing penance there, and leading a celeftial life, till he made a moft holy end.

The Saints therfore haue well vnderftood, the danger which ordinarily there is in human praife; efpecially when they are giuen with great honour, and eftimation of fanctity. And for this reafon , when we praife the feruants of God, for the benefit of others, wee are to doe it , if wee can, in their abfence.

Wee are alfo to doe fo , for an other reafon, which is, to fecure
our

our felues from the note and fufpicion of being flatterers . For
when wee praife our neighbour,
for the profit of his foule, namely
to deliuer him from pufillani-
mity, and to animate him to vertue, the neceffity which then ther
is of praifing him in his prefence,
will free vs from being fufpected
to doe it our of flattery: but when
wee praife him for the good of
others, if wee doe it without ne-
eeffity in his prefence, it draweth
the fufpicion of flattery with it;
and therefore as much as we may,
wee muft procure to giue fuch
praife in abfence . And this alfo
did *Chrift* our Lord teach vs , in
this praife of Saint *Iohn.* For vpõ
this reafon , he ftaied till the difciples of the Saint were gone, to
auoid all fufpicion of flattery. So
faid Saint *Chryfoftome;* Therefore
did *Chrift* our Lord praife Saint

Iohn, whē his difciples were gone,
that fo it might not feeme to be
flattery.

THE XXIV. CHAPTER.

Of other rules which wee muft ob-
ferue when wee praife men: that is,
that wee praife fome , without of-
fence to others : and that wee doeit
in moderate words.

ANother rule which wee are
to obferue in thefe praifes,
is to praife fome in fuch forte, as
that we giue no offence to others,
by diminifhing the vertues and
parts of fome , to encreafe thofe
of other folkes. And therefore we
muft procure as much as we may,
not to make cōparifons between
fome and others ; telling the
faultes of this man, and the abilities of that other; abafing and
vili-

vilifying fome, and exalting and
magnifying other men; and of
this we muft efpecially take heed,
when they of whom wee fpeake,
are aliue.

Chrift our Lord gaue vs an example of this rule, in the praife
which he vttered of Saint *Iohn*;
for he faid not of him that he was
*the greateft of all them who had been
borne of woemen; but that no man had
been borne before that time, greater
then hee*; thereby leauing men in
liberty, to thinke that others,
might be equall to him. And out
of this general fetéce, he brought
that exception which was fit, faying, *that the leaft of the kingdome of
heauen was greater then he.* And although fome vnderftand thereby
the leaft of the Angells, who are
bleffed in heauen; yet the more
certaine expofition is (as we haue
faid before) that he vnderftood
him

him who was *the least*, by humility, which is, that Saint of Saints;
and he who is the fountaine of all
sanctity, of whom Saint *Iohn Baptist* himselfe said, *that he was not
worthy to vntie the latchet of his shoo.*

Wee also must follow this rule
of prudence in praising men, who
are praise worthy. For if we praise
men for the loue of God, & being
moued by charity as wee ought;
the same charity will tell vs, that
we must doe it without offending
any body, and that so wee must
comfort, and honour some with
our praise, as that wee doe not
offend, or dispraise others by
sleighting their vertues.

The last rule which wee are to
hold is that wee praise men, euen
although they be Saints, with
moderation, and temperance, &
in modest wordes; in such sorte
that wee exceed not the limits,
either

either of truth, or of necessity, by
our enforcing, or exaggeration
thereof. For if wee praise a man,
either to make him friendly, or
to animate him to the doing of
good, or to perswade him to the
beleefe of any truth, or to the
practise of any vertue, or to
gaine credit for him with other
folkes; it will be fit to speake so
well of him as is necessary, for the
obtaining of that end, which is
pretended, & to worke that good
effect which is desired; and this is
sufficient, laying other praises
and exaggerations aside, which
neither are necessary, nor profitable to the edification of others.

This moderation which wee
ought to vse in praising men, is
taught vs by the holy Scripture
saying, *doe not praise a man, till he
be dead.* He doth not here prohi-
bite all praise of such as liue; for

it

it is clearly lawful, and necessary, and pleasing to God, to praise men, whilest they liue, as we haue declared already; and the Scripture it selfe saith; *The faithfull man, shall be much praised*. But he meaneth, that wee must not praise such as are still liuing, with a cōpleat and perfect praise, as if they were secure, and confirmed in the state of grace, as they are to be, in heauen. And so that, *doe not praise*, doth signify as the Greeke letter sheweth; *do not beatify or proclame any man for blessed before his death*: which sentence grew into this Prouerbe; *Let no man coūt himselfe happy before he dy*. And therfore wee are admonished by this sentence, not to praise any man, as absolutely blessed, or entirely happy in this life: but when wee say *he is happy*, wee are to vnderstand it with this condition or li-

mita-

mitation; that he is happy according to the present iustice, wherin he liues; or happy according to
his present state and disposition:
and, in fine, that he is happy in
hope. For as long as a man liueth,
it is euer fit for him to be affraid
of falling, and to be in doubt of
perseuering. Yet this takes not
from vs, but that wee may praise
good men; but onely that our
praise of thē must be moderate, as
of mē who may faile in the course
of vertue, wherin they are; & may
fall vpō that sinne in which they
are not; til the good ēd of a happy
death, doe secure their vertue, &
ratify their good life. This did
S. *Ambrose* declare in these words;
*He is not instantly happy, who hath
now no sinne in his soule; for it is not
said without cause, that we must praise
no man before his death.* And it is certaine that whilest a man liues, he
may

may faile; and therefore till he
dy, he muſt not be celebrated
with any praiſe, as determinate
and certaine, and which cannot
be reuoked. He, who after the end
of a good life, hath died well, may
be iuſtly termed happy: for already he enioyeth the ſociety of
the bleſſed, with a ſecurity, which
is perfect.

THE XXV. CHAPTER.

*Of the rules, which they are to keepe,
who are praiſed; that ſo they may
be at no preiudice, but receiue profit
thereby.*

THey who praiſe others, are
to obſerue thoſe rules, wherof I haue ſpoken. Let vs now ſay
ſomewhat, of the rules which are
to be kept by them, who are praiſed; remitting the reſt to ſome
other

other place.

The firſt rule is , that a man (for as much as concernes him-ſelfe, that is to ſay, his owne ho-nour, his eſtimation and his com-fort) muſt not deſire or ſeeke the praiſe of men. For to deſire praiſe vpon theſe reaſons , and for this end is a vaine and vitious thing, which ſpotteth , and defileth the heart of man, and diſquieteth and diſturbeth it, and maketh it ſub-ject to euery change . For as all human thinges are ſubiect to al-teration; and one man praiſeth, and another man diſpraiſeth; one exalteth , and another abaſeth; one honoureth, and another diſ-honoureth his neighbour: from hence it groweth, that the miſe-rable heart, which loueth praiſe, is now cheerfull , and then ſad; now refreſhed & them diſmaied; and neuer doth enioy ſtrength or reſt.

reſt. On the other a má who cares
not for the praiſes of men, but
deſpiſeth and auoides them; and,
for his part, deſireth onely to be
approoued, and praiſed by Almighty God, whoſe iudgment is
right, and vpon whoſe approbation and praiſe, our ſaluation dependeth, and who contents himſelfe with this teſtimony, doth
proceed like a iuſt man, who loue-
eth true iuſtice, and not vanity;
and ſo keepes his heart quiet, and
firmely ſet vpō goodnes, becauſe
he reſteth himſelf vpon God, who
is not ſubiect to any change. So
ſaith Saint *Chryſoſtome.* The wicked man is delighted with the
praiſes of men, and though he
haue not the vertue, for which
he is praiſed, yet he holds his
peace, and is glad of it. But the
iuſt man flies from praiſe, and
though he haue that vertue for
which

which they praise him, & though
he know thereby, that he who
praised him, said true; yet still he
hath no minde to be praised. And
in another place, the same Saint
faith ; Nothing makes men so
vaine, and light, as the appetite
of glory, & of the praise of men,
and so nothing maketh them so
firme and conſtant , and ſtrong,
as the cōtempt of all the honour,
and praise of this world.

But now ſince it is not lawfull
to like the praises of men for his
owne honour, and temporal comfort; let vs see, whether it be lawfull for him to like, and deſire
them for the animating, and encouraging himſelfe thereby, to
the exerciſe of vertue. We therfore ſay firſt, that this may bee
lawfull in ſome caſe , and with
ſome moderation; as namely for
a man, who is in affliction, or de-
ſola-

folation, to defire that men may
comfort him; putting him in
minde of the good he hath done,
or of the fruite which hath followed vpon his actions, or by his
example or inftruction: that fo he
may not be difmaied with his affliction; and if he be difmaied,
that he may take heart: not ad-
mitting of that praife with any
meaning to dwell therein; but as
a receipt of phyficke, wherewith
to cure his infirmity, and weaknes; and to induce himfelfe the
better to ferue God, for what
God is, and for the accomplifh-
ment of his holy will. As King
Ezechias did, who being in the extreamity of ficknes, and much
afflicted with the approach of
death, did for the increafe of his
confidence in God, and for the
comfort of his foule, and the re-
dreffe of his defolation, comme-
morate

morate to God himſelf, the good
deedes he had done, ſaying thus;
I beſeech thee, ô Lord remember
how I haue liued , and conuerſed
before thee, with truth, and without all hypocriſy or diſſimula-
tion; & how in all things which
concerned thy Religion , I haue
ſerued thee with the intire affection of my heart; not honouring
any other God, but thee, who art
the true God; and how I haue performed theſe good workes which
thou haſt commaunded . In this
ſort the good afflicted King , ac-
knowledging that all the good
things which he had done, were
the gifts of God , and referring
them all to him, reduced them to
his memory, and preſented them
before almighty God; not reſting
and relying vpon them; but vpon
the mercy and grace of God ; by
meanes whereof he had wrought
them;

them: & he did it to the end that he might erect himselfe to some good hope ; and to comfort his sad heart . And so it may be lawfull for an afflicted man, with the same intention , and to the same end , to like and accept of being assisted by this meanes of the pious , and confortable speech of his neighbour.

Secondly we say, that although this manner of praise may be lawfully accepted with this moderation : yet it is not conuenient to desire, or procure it; because there are many better meanes thē this, whereby to be animated, and induced to vertue; and by reason of danger which there is , in louing humane praise , and the honour which growes therby; and of making value , and taking complacence in himselfe, and so grow to do well for the honours sake. And

because

becaufe this inconuenience and
hurt groweth ordinarily vpon
them who defire to be praifed for
this end ; Saint *Gregory* condénes
it,faying; It as a thing which belongeth to arrogant perfons,and
giuen to vanity , when they defire to be animated to doe well,
by the praifes of others . And
preachers and inftructers of o-
thers , who for this reafon defire
praife , are difmaied , when they
are not praifed; and being ambitious louers of humane honour
and fauour, they will defend and
excufe themfelues faying,that it
is lawfull for them to defire it,
for the good which they receiue
by humane praife ; and for this,
they fhew their abilities,and will
be praifed for them , to the end
that by meanes of this praife,
they may growe more in vertue.
Whereby certainly they deceiue

N　　them-

themselues, and so by meanes of
this errour, that disteper increa-
seth in them, by which they loue
and desire the praise of men. But
the true seruants of God, are free
from this vanity; for although
they labour by their vertues, to
equal the praises, wherewith men
celebrate the same, yet they desire not to be praised by men, but
they despise praise, with their
heart; and for asmuch as concerneth themselues they flie from it
with great earnestnes. Thus saith
Saint *Gregory.* Whereupon it followeth clearly, that it is not conuenient, for the end of profiting
our selues, to desire the praise of
men, by reason of the deceit, and
danger which lyeth hid therein,
that wee may not perhaps doe it
for any true necessity, but for vanity; and not for the true profit
of our soules, but to the preiudice
ther-

thereof.

The intention & end for which
wee may lawfully defire, or admit
of praife , is for the good of our
neighbours ; to the end that by
the conceit , and good opinion,
which they haue of our life and
doctrine, they may grow the better by vs; edifying themfelues by
our good example, and inducing
themfelues to the loue of vertue,
by meanes of our aduice and
counfelle, or of our gouernment,
or doctrine. So faith the glorious
Saint *Auguftine.* He who worketh
according to vertue defireth not
praife : but yet praife ought to
follow him , who worketh well;
to the end that it may profit thē,
who praife, by encouraging thē-
felues to the vertues, which they
praife. But howfoeuer it be lawfull to defire praife for this end,
becaufe in this cafe , it is not

praife which is loued and defired, but the profit of their neighbours ; yet the better and more
fecure way, and that which hath
been vfed by the Saints , is ; not
to procure or defire, euen for this
very end, to be praifed by men;
nor that men fhould publifh his
vertues and celebrate him for the
fame, leaft fome vanity or other,
giue it felfe to his foule; but that
he leaue it to Gods prouidence,
that fo he may doe therein, as he
fhall thinke moft fit, and defiring
(for as much as cōcernes himfelf)
that he be not praifed.

The thing which he is to doe,
is that he labour hard , and bee
watchfull in doing good & holy
workes; & in giuing good example in all thinges, and vfing holy
difcourfe, & teaching found doctrine, and giuing wholfome aduice, and defiring , that the men
who

who shall happen to see his good
workes, and to heare his good
wordes, may be stirred vp to
know, that God is the Author of
them, and may praise him for
them, and be induced to serue
him, performing not onely those
workes which he doth and teacheth, but others which may be
much better. And when he shall
find or vnderstãd, that men praise
him, for what he doth, let him
enter into his owne heart, and
despise himselfe through the
knowledge he hath of his sinnes;
for which he deserueth all contempt; and let him hold himselfe vnworthy of such praise, for
hauing offended God, who was
the principall Author of those
good workes. And let him desire,
that men, forgetting or despi-
sing him, as he deserueth, may
giue the praise and glory of those

N 3 good

good workes of God. To this are
wee aduifed by Saint *Auguſtine,* in
thefe wordes. The praife which is
giuen to a iuſt man, for the good
he doth, he muſt inſtantly referre
to God; defiring that his diuine
Maieſty, who is the Authour of
that good worke, may be praifed
for it; for the men who are good,
haue not their being fo, from thé-
felues, but from God. And when
mé praife vs, let vs reforme thofe
praifes, giuing all to God, who
gaue vs that goodnes, which is
praifed by men. And in an other
place, the fame Saint faith, when
thou ſhalt be praifed, defpife thy
felfe, and defire that he may be
praifed in thee, who worketh in
thee, the good thou doeſt; and fo
thou muſt not doe good thinges
for thine owne praife, but for the
praife of that Lord, of whom thou
didſt receiue the good thou doeſt.
                                    And

And heerwith wee will conclude
the rules which are to be obserued, both by such as praise , and
such as are praised.

And so also will wee conclude
our discourse , concerning those
thinges which belong to the most
sweet vertue of *Benignity* , and
which in summe are these. To do
good to our neighbours with liberality, & with a willing minde;
To graunt them with ease, what
they aske; To condescēd to them
in things lawfull; To coūerse affably and sweetly; and both in
countenance and wordes , to be
cheerfull; To indure meekly the
defects of others ; To reprehend
them with loue; To pardon them
with mercy ; To impose com-
maundments vpon such as are
subiect , which they may obey
with gust; and to impose burdens
on them which they may carry
                                with

with eafe; To be curteous and wel
mannered; And to praife the vertue of others for the comfort, &
edification and fpiritual profit of
our neighbours.

By the practife of this vertue,
wee fhall growe moft like to God,
who is moft *Benigne*; and we fhall
become acceptable to his moft
pitteous heart, and moreouer we
fhall prooue pleafing and agreeable to good men, for their edification; & more tolerable to wicked men, for the conuerfion and
winning of their foules to God.
And hereby wee fhall alfo mor-
tify thofe inclinatiõs in vs, which
are contrary to *Benignity*, and fo
obtaine victory ouer our felues;
and we fhall exercife many moft
excellent acts of other vertues,
which carry relation, and refpect
to *Benignity*; and wee fhall obteine
great peace & quietnes of heart,
wher-

wherby we may the better be difpofed to communicate with Almighty God, by meanes of Prayer, and Contemplation.

And finally , if wee will exercife *Benignity* towards our neighbours, we fhall haue more perfect
experience of the *Benignity* of
God, through the abundant gift
of fpiritual graces and comforts,
which he will impart to vs . And
aboue all thinges , wee fhall be
enabled heerby, to performe his
holy wil; therby doing that which
he comaundeth vs, by his Bleffed
Apoftle faying, *Ephef.*4. *Be you Benigne one towards another*; *Be mercifull, hauing compaffion of one anothers
mifery* ; *and pardoning all iniuries to
one another*, *in fuch fort as God hath
pardoned vs, by the vertue and merit of
Chrift our Lord.*

F I N I S.

MATTHEW WILSON

A Direction to be Observed by N. N.

1636

A
DIRECTION
TO BE OBSERVED
By N. N.

If hee meane to proceede in Answering the Booke intituled
Mercy and *Truth*, or *Charity Maintained* by
Catholiks &c.

*For I say by the grace that is giuen me,
to all that are among you, not to be
more wise then behoueth to be wise,
but to be wise vnto sobrietie.* Ad
Roman. 12. v. 3.

When we treate of religion, that is,
of the worship and knowledge of
God, they are least to be followed, who promising most liberally
proofes by *reason*, forbid vs to belieue. *S. Aug. De vtil. Cred. cap. 12.*

Permissu Superiorum, 1636.

A
DIRECTION
TO BE OBSERVED
By N. N.

If he meane to proceede in Answering
the Booke intituled *Mercy* and
Truth, or, *Charity Maintained* by Catholiks &c.

IN regard that hee, who pretends to be answering the
Booke intituled *Mercy and
Truth*, or, *Charity Maintained* by Catholicks &c: Is strongly
reported to be a *Socinian* : before I
giue him his *charge*, it will be requisite,
to open in brief, what kinde of people
they be, who haue appeared of late
vnder the name of *Socinians*. For by
this meanes, it will be seene, whether
his true intention be, to defend *Protestantisme*, or couertly to vent *Socini-*

anisme

anifme. It will also appeare, whether all his paines be taken to any purpose. For *Charity Maintained* hauing been written against *Proteftants*, not intermedling with the Doctrine of *Socinians*, he will neuer by thought to fpeake one word to the purpose against that Booke, if he anfwer out of Principles, which *Proteftants* themfelues will profeffe to deteft, no leffe then *Catholicks* doe.

CHAP. I.

Of Socinianifme.

SOcinians take their name from one *Fauftus Socinus*, an Italian Apoftata, that is, vpon the matter, an Atheift. For they are ftrangers to that wife and gallant Nation, who imagine, they can be of any Religion, if they will not be Catholicks. The maine and capitall doctrine of perfect *Socinians*, is, rather Negatiue, and deftructiue of all Faith and Religion, then pofitiue or Affirmatiue of any one.

one. The Summe of all is this. Nothing ought, or can be certainly belieued, further then it may be proued by euidence of naturall reason, into which they resolue all Christian (a) Faith. Out of this vniuersall ground, they doe, and must (if they will speake as they thinke, and thinke according to their owne principles) reiect all *infallible*, *supernaturall*, *infused Faith*, which they reduce to meere *humane knowledge*, or *opinion*. And this the *Answerer*, as I am *told*, professes, and endeauours to proue. They must then affirme, that *Faith* is not *donum Dei*, an especiall gift of God; but only the common light of Reason, or habits acquired by a mans owne abilitie and industrie. Diuine *Faith* being excluded, the other two Theologicall infused vertues, *Hope*, and *Charitie*, cannot subsiste. All infused Reuelations, and Prophecies; all Illuminations, and Inspirations of the Holy Ghost; all preuenient, concomitant, subsequent, and, in a word, all kind of whatsoeuer *supernaturall Grace*, is derided by this gracelesse *Sect*.

(a) Irenæus Philalethes lib. cuj titulus: Disquisitio breuis &c. S. Aug. De vtil. Cred. cap. 1. Nosti enim Honorate, non aliam ob causam nos in tales homines (Manichæos) incidisse, nisi quod se dicebant terribili authoritate separata, mira ac simplici ratione eos qui se audire vellent in introducturos ad Deum, & errore omni liberaturos.

And

And as they denie all supernaturall Faith, so doe they laugh at the beliefe of all obiects, that are beyond the sphere of naturall discourse. And therfore they vtterly denie (b) the most Blessed Trinity, the Incarnation of the Sonne of God, the Godhead of our deare Sauiour Christ, his satisfaction for the sinnes of men, and his (c) merit (and to proue this, they bring the same arguments, which Protestants were wont to vrge against the merits of iust men, and works of supererogation) the Diuinitie of the (d) Holy Ghost, and Originall (e) sinne. Eternall supernaturall Felicitie in Heauen for the Iust, and endlesse punishment in Hell for the wicked, they all must, according to their Principles, & some of them doe roundly denie. And they cannot place their last Happines in any thing, except some such poore ima ginarie good, as old Pagan Philosophers dreamed of, but could neuer attaine, nor so much as agree among themselues, wherin it consisted.

They denie the Resurrection of our Bodies, and teach, that our Soule is to

be

(b) Ioan.
Volkelius
de vera
Religione
lib. 5. c.
9.10.11.
12. 13.
(c) Idem.
ibid. c.
20. 22.
(d) Id. v.
bi supra.
cap. 14.
(e) Id. i-
bid. cap.
15.

be ioyned with a Celestiall or spirituall substance, of a nature essentially
different from these our earthlie bodies; and that our Blessed Sauiour in
Heauen, hath such a Celestiall (f) *(f) Vol-*
Bodie. *kel. l. 3.*

That the world was created in *time*, *c. 35.*
by the free decree of God, & not from
Eternitie, by a necessarie emanation
from him, they belieue no more, then
can be proued by euidence of naturall
demonstration. And I know some of
them hold, directly against holie Scripture, that it was from all eternitie, by
such a necessarie resultancie, as that.

They make small reckoning of *Sa-*
craments, as being, according to them,
neither *signes*, nor *seales*, nor *causes* of
of *grace*; which *grace*, they hold to be
a meere fiction. Yea they teach, that
it is an abuse of the word *Sacrament*, to
apply it to (g) *holy rites*. And as for the *(g) Vol-*
Eucharist in particular, one of their *kel. l. 4.*
ring leaders teacheth, that it is no (h) *cap. 22.*
Sacrament; that for the matter there- (h) *Ibid,*
of, if one cannot drinke wine, hee may
vse (i) water, without changing the (i) *Ibid.*
substance of the Lord's Supper (as he
                                    speakes)

speakes) and that it may be admini-
stred by Lay (*k*) Persons ; and receaued euen by such, as are not (*l*) Bapti-
zed.

The same prime *Socinian* denies Baptisme to be a Sacrament, and teacheth,
that all are not obliged to receaue it,
but that some may be enrolled amongst
the number of Christians, without it;
that the Church may either leaue it
off, or at least can compell none to receaue it ; and, in a word, that it is a
a thing but adiaphorous, or indifferent ; with other wicked (*m*) absurdi-
ties, which I let passe.

Concerning holie Scripture ; to
such persons, as they hold not fit to
be intirely trusted by them, they will
acknowledge them all ; before other
more confident friends, they reiect
diuers parts of holy Scripture, receaued euen in the Protestant Church of
England; and with men, who are fully
acquainted with their Principles, they
must hold, not any one Book, Chapter,
or line of the whole Old and New
Testament, to be the word of God, or
written by the infallible assistance in-
spiration,

(k) *Ibid.*
(l) *Lib.*
6. *cap.*
14.

(m) *Vide*
Volkel.
lib.cap.6.
c. 14. per
totum.

spiration, and direction of his holy
Spirit. For naturall reason, which with
them is the sole *Rule* of *Faith*, & *Iudge*
of all *Controuersies*, cannot possibly
demonstrate these things. They may
belieue by a kind of Humane Faith,
that the Books of holy Scripture were
written by such particular men (as
they belieue the Workes of *Plato*,
Tullie, *Linie*, to be theirs) but that
those men were endued *with* an *vniuer-*
sall infallibilitie, euen in writing Scripture, they neither doe; nor can affirme, (n) *Volk.*
but rather teach the (*n*) contrarie.   *l. 5. c. 5.*

 Neither yet doth their impietie stay (o) *Io.*
here, but one of them dares (*o*) affirme, *Crellius*
that God could not know from Eter- *lib. de*
nitie *futura contingentia*, such things, *Deo, &*
as doe proceede from Free-Will, and *Attri-*
election; which is in effect, to take *butis eius*
away all infallible predictions pro- *c.* 24.
phecies of voluntarie free actions.
And out of this grosse errour, some o-
ther more open *Socinian*, will proceed
to the deniall of God himselfe. For
how can God be, and be God, ans
yet be ignorant of any thing, that is
possible, past, present, or to come ?
           If

If you aske these men, what they meane by the true Church; they must answer, that there is no other true Church, but all Mankinde, as it agrees in the light of naturall reason; and that there is no ether authoritie, to which a man is obliged to submit.

If againe you inquire, in what *Heresie* doth indeed consiste; they replie, that it consistes only in opposing the dictamen, or iudgement of a man's owne reason. They might as well say in plaine termes : There is no such thing, as Christians are wont to call *Heresie*. For it is impossible, that a man iudge contrarie to that, which he iudgeth. *Intellectus non est hypocrita.* Our vnderstanding cannot play the hypocrite with it self. A man's hands, lookes, words, or writing may belie his thoughts, and make him deserue the name of dissembler, falsifier, hypocrite. But it implies a manifest contradiction, that our internall thoughts should tell vs, at the same time, that a thing is both so, and not so; and therefore, according to their large definition, there can be no *Heresie* at all.

And

And their assertions tending to *practise*, are agreable to this their *specula-
tion*. For they teach, that no man ought
now to be punished, either spiritually
by (p) Excommunication, or (q) tem-
porally, with the losse of goods, im-
prisonment, or death, as long as he
followes the dictamen of his owne
Conscience; though otherwise he
denie Articles belieued by all good
Christians; as for example, concerning
the most Blessed Trinity, the Diuinity,
of Christ our Lord, Originall sinne &c.

But why doe I specifie particulars,
which would be infinite? For whatsoeuer our Sauiour Christ, his holy
Apostles, the Catholicke Church,
Councels, Fathers, Doctours, Diuines,
Christians, propose to be belieued a-
boue humane reason, or with a *supernaturall infallible* assent, is, to these
men, no other then a fiction, an impe-
sture, an impossibilitie. *Diuinity*, with
them, can be nothing but *Philosophie.
Reason* alone is *Faith*; *Sanctitie* consistes only in *Moralitie*. *Plato*, or *Ari-
stotle*, or any other, must be as soone
belieued, as the testimonie of our deare
Sauiour;

(p) Iren.
Philalethes
lib. cui titu-
lus: Differ-
tatio de Pace
Ecclesia.

(q) *Vol-
kel. lib.6.
cap.* 15.

14

Sauiour; vnles he proue what he saith, by better reason, the other do. *(r)* What Christian can heare these infidelities, without detestation? What Church can tolerate them, and yet pretend zeale in Religion? Neuertheles, this vngodlie *sect* spreades it selfe, being cunningly obtruded by some (and by the *Answerer* in particular) & greedily swallowed by many, and duly punished by none; although I ought not to dissemble, but doe gladly acknowledge, and deseruedly publish in this occasion, for a patterne to other in this Realme, the care of the chiefest Prelate in *England*, in prohibiting the sale of Bookes tending to *Socinianisme*. Let men in the meane time speake their pleasure, against the vigilancie of Prelats in Catholicke Countries; against the seueritie of Ecclesiasticall Canons; against forbidding to reade pernicious bookes; against the *Index Expurgatorius*, and against the holie Office of *Inquisition* in Italie, and some other places. Sure I am, through want of such holesome meanes *Heresies*, *Infidelities*, and *Atheismes*,

(r) Si autem Christo etiam credendum negant, nisi indubitata ratio reddita fuerit, Christiani non sunt. Nam id aduersus nos Pagani quidam dicunt, stultè quidem, sed non sibi aduersi, nec repugnantes. Hos vero quis feratad Christum se pertinere profiteri, qui nisi apertissimam rationem stultis de Deo protulerint, nihil credendum esse contendunt? S. Aug. De vtil. Cred. cap. 14

ismes, are hatched, & receaue growth; and innumerable soules eternally perish. And because the Reader may well remaine in wonder, how so very absurd errours, can possibly finde entertainement among Christians; it will not by impertinent, though besides my first intention, to set downe some reasons thereof, as they now present themselues to my minde. And they may serue for the argument of the ensuing Chapter.

CHAP. II.

Some reasons, why so many embrace Socinianisme.

TO omit, that this Heresie giue full scope to euerie man's *vnderstanding*, to belieue, as his fancie shall dictate, and for his will, to sinne without feare of eternall punishment (yea and not to belieue, that there is a God, if some licentious impe can obiect against the Diuine Existence, Prouidence, Iustice, Mercie, Wisdome, or other Attributes an
argu-

argument, which he cannot folue, and maifter the wit of whatfoeuer Atheift) I will, for the prefent, touch only foure reafons, drawne : *firft*, from the doctrine of Proteftants; *fecondly*, from the practife of the Church of England, ioyned with the difpofition of Socinians; *thirdly*, from the perfonall qualitie of Proteftant Diuines; *fourthly*, from fome circumftances of perfons, time, and place.

First then, I fay, that the verie Doctrine of Proteftants if it be followed clofely, and with coherence to it felf, muft of necefsitie induce *Socinianifme*. This I fay confidently, and euidently proue, by inftancing in one errour, which may well be tearmed the Capitall, and mother Herefie, from which, all other muft follow at eafe; I meane, their herefie in affirming, that the perpetually vifible Church of Chrift, defcended by a neuer interrupted fucefsion from our Sauiour, to this day, is not infallible in all that it propofeth to be belieued, as reuealed truths.

For if the *infallibilitie* of fuch a publicke *Authoritie* be once impeached;

what

S. Aug. De vtil. Cred. c. 16. Sola eft authoritas quæ commouet ftultos vt ad fapientiam feftinent. Quandiu intelligere fynceranon poffumus, authoritate quidem decipi miferum eft: fed certè miferius non moueri. Si enim Dei prouidentia

what remaines, but that euerie man is giuen ouer to his owne *wit*, and *dif-course*? And talke not here, of holy Scripture. For if the true Church may erre, in defining, what Scriptures be Canonicall; or in deliuering the fenfe and meaning thereof; we are ftill de-uolued, either vpon the *priuate fpirit* (a foolerie now exploded out of Eng-land, which finally leauing euery man to his owne conceits, ends in *So-cinianifme*) or els vpon naturall wit, and iudgement, for examining and determining, what Scriptures con-taine true or falfe doctrine, and in that refpect, ought to bee receaued, or reiected. And indeed, take away the authority of Gods Church, no man can bee affured, that any one Booke, or parcell of Scripture, was written by diuine infpiration; or that all the contents, are infallibly true; which are the direct errours of *Soci-mians*. If it were but for this reafon alone, no man, who regardes the eternall faluation of his foule, would liue or dye in *Proteftancie*, from which, fo vafte abfurdities, as thefe of the *So-*

non præfidæ rebus huma-nis, nihil eft de religione fatagendum. Sin vero & fpecies re-rum omni-um, quam profecto ex aliquo verif-fimæ pul-chritudinis fonte manad re redden-dum eft; & interiori nefcio qua confcientia Deum quæ-rendum, Deoque fer-uiendum, meliores quofque animos quæ-fi publice priuatimque hortatur: non eft de-fperandum ab eodem ipfo Deo au-thoritatem aliquam conftitutam, qua velut gradu certo innitentes, attollamur in Deum.

B *cinians,*

cinians must ineuitably follow. And it ought to be an vnspeakable comfort to all vs Catholicks, while we consider, that none can denie the infallible authoritie of our Church, but ioyntly he must be left to his owne wit, and waies; and must abandon all *infused Faith*, and true Religion, if he doe but vnderstand himselfe aright.

The second reason, drawne from the proceeding of the Church of *England*, I vnderstand to be, that their ayme and industrie, tendes only to procure an exteriour conformitie to the Lawes of the Realme. In so much, that, if a Catholicke, for example, would resort to their Church Seruice, and Sermons; take Oath of Supremacie; receaue their Communion, and abiure the Catholicke Faith, though withall he protest to doe it only for feare, and against his Conscience; yea and that he dislikes their Seruice, Sermons, Faith, and Communion: In this case, they are, and must be satisfied with the forced actions of such a miserable man, though euen his owne roung beare witnesses, that all is donne against his conscience. And what is this, but to neglect the Soule, vpon condition, to receaue some kinde of violent tribute from the Bodie? This then being the spirit of the *English* Church, on the one side; and *Socinians*, on the other, making no scruple (with what honestie, I leaue to be considered) to sorte themselues, for the exteriour, with what Religion soeuer; no wonder, if by this meanes, they haue a large scope, to instill their Doctrine; and yet walke with as much freedome, as any Protestant can doe.

The third reason, taken from the qualitie of Protestant Diuines is this Socinians destroying all *supernaturell* beliefe, or *infallible* assent, to any Object, surpassing the reach of Humane Reason, haue as manie, and as strong obiections readie at hand, against the Articles of our Faith, as the weake vnderstanding of man doth finde difficulties, in the knowledge of Diuines things. Now, the learning of *Protestant* Diuines, consisting

only

onely in some superficiall talent of
Preaching, languages, or elocution,
& not in any deep knowledge of *Philosophie*, especially of *Metaphisicke*, and
much lesse of that most solide, profitable, subtile, and succinct method, which
wee call *Schoole Diuinitie*; when they
come to be pressed by *Socinians*, are vn-
able to satisfie their doubts, but either
are caught themselues, as I know it
hapneth not seldome; or giue occasion
for the *Socinians* to be more setled in
their errours ; and for others to be
drawne into the same infidelitie. And
the Diuell aymed at no lesse then this
totall ruine of all Faith and Religion,
when he first moued Hereticks to de-
ride *Schoole Diuinitie*, and to nickname
the Professours thereof, dunses.

The fourth reason, that casts so manie, especially, of the best wits, vpon
Socinianisme, both Diuines, and other
among Protestants, is, because they
will not be Catholicks *in these times* ;
they *cannot* bring their vnderstanding
to be Protestants; and so they take the
large and easie way of belieuing, what
they list. And, to speake the truth,

what

what learned iudicious man, can,
after vnpartiall examination, imbrace
Proteſtantiſme? which waxeth euen
wearie of it ſelf (and this is an infallible marke of Sects and Hereſies; for
where the Holy Ghoſt Directeth,
there can bee no contrarieties, or mu-
tabilitie) its Profeſſours, they eſpecially of greateſt worth, learning,
and authoritie, declare themſelues to
loue temper and moderation, allowe
of manie things, which ſome yeares
agoe were vſually condemned, as ſu-
perſtitious and Antichriſtian; and are
at this time more vnreſolued where to
faſten, then at the infancie of their
Church. Thus *Truth*, the Center of
our vnderſtanding, maugre neuer ſo
long, or ſtrong oppoſition, worketh
powerfully, though patiently, and
by inſenſible degrees, calls men backe
from fierceneſſe to doubtfulneſſe, from
doubtfulneſſe to certaintie, that at
length they may ioy in a ſetled con-
ſtancie. And in this it is very appa-
rent, that the Holy Ghoſt directs the
Church of *Rome*; which proceeding
alwayes vpon the ſame grounds, and

believing

believing, that Christ our Lord is still present with his Spouse, ascribes as much infallibilitie to the present Church, as to that of the first fiue hundred yeares; and reuerenceth the late Councell of *Trent*, no lesse then the ancient Councell of *Nice*. For the promises of our deare Sauiour, were not limited for any Age; without the afsistance of whose holy Spirit, no times, or persons, are exempted from errours; and with it, all are sure not to erre. And this is the true reason, why the *Romm* Church is still the same, without opposition to it selfe in any least Doctrine; whereas all other Sects, and Sectaries, are notoriously knowne, to contradict both their Afsociats, and themselues, as now I was saying of the Protestant Church in *England*. For doe not their Churches beginne to looke with another face? their walles to speake a new language? their Preachers to vse a sweeter tone? their annuall publicke Tenets, in their Vniuersities, to be of another stile, & matter? their bookes to appeare with titles and arguments, which once would haue

haue caufed a mightie fcandall among the Brethren ? their Doctrine to be altered in manie things , (*a*) and euen in thofe verie points , for which their Progenitours forfooke the then vifible Church of Chrift ? Their 39. *Articles* that is , the fumme, the Confefsion, & almoft the Creede of their Faith , are patient; patient? they are ambitious of fome fenfe, wherein they may feeme to bé Catholick. To alledge the necefsitie of wife and children in thefe dayes , is but a weake plea , for a married Minifter , to compaffe a Benefice. Firie *Caluinifme* , once a darling in *England*, is at lenght accounted Herefie; yea and little leffe then Treafon men, in word and writing , vfe willingly the once fearfull names of *Priefts*, and *Altars*. Nay if one dœ but mutter againft the placing of the Altar after the old fafhion, for a warning he fhall be well warmed by (*b*) *a Coale from the Altar*. Englifh Proteftants are now put in (*c*) minde that for expofition of Scripture ,

(*a*) For ex-ample , the Pope not Antichrift; Prayer for the Dead; Limbus Patrum; Pictures; that the Church hath authoritie to determine Controuerfies in Faith, and to interpret the Scripture; about Freewill, and Predeftination; Vniuerfall Grace; that al our works are not fins; merit of goodworks; inherent Iuftice; Faith alone doth not iuftifie; Charitie is to be preferred before knowledge: Traditions; Commandements poffible to bee

kept, &c. (b) A little Treatife fo intituled , & printed An. 1636.
(c) Sunday no Sabbath. A Sermon printed An. 1636 pag. 38.

B 4   by

(d) *Lib. Can. An.* 1571. *Can.* 19.

by (d) *Canon they are bound to follow* the ancient Fathers ; which if they doe with sinceritie, euery learned Prote-stant Diuine, who makes a conscience to belie his owne knowledge, can tell, what doome will passe against Prote-stancie, euen by confession of Prote-stants themselues, as the *Answerer* once auouched (as shall appeare here-after *Chap.* 5. *n.* 6.) and this being only a matter of *fact*, and requiring no more then reading, and vnderstan-ding the toungs, wherein the Fathers wrote, or the Translations of their Works, he cannot in morall honestie, and therefore, I hope, will not, gain-say his own words; nor can be thought to speake sincerely, if hee should for-cedly now retract, what then he freely wrote. And I know, that to some Pro-testants, hee so cleerely demonstrated, the Fathers to bee on our side, that they remained conuineed, and haue vpon occasion acknowledged no lesse. But let vs goe on. The foure prime *Protestant Church-Chroniclers*, who pretend to deduce a succession of the true Church (the *Centurists*, I meane) are

are without ceremonie demanded in a *particular* occasion : *with what face dare they vente such vntruths?* and *with what conscience dare they* (e) *forge &c.* their bad carriage towards the ancient Fathers is displayd ; and for a *generall* Censure, they are told, that *Their credit is eclipsed, and their testimonie abated by their* (f) *doings.* And to conclude all in one maine point. The *Protestant* Church in *England*, willingly professeth so small Antiquitie, and so weake subsistance in it selfe, that they acknowledge no other visible being for many Ages ; but in the Church of *Rome.* Which *position* drawne from them by meere necessitie, must force them to yeeld, that the *Roman* Church doth not erre in any point necessarie to Saluation, vnlesse they haue a minde, to bee telling the world, that in their owne Church, for many Ages, none could be saued. They must therefore bee still content, to heare vs tell them againe and againe, this most necessary truth. You cannot bee saued, vnlesse you belieue, that wee in our Church are capable of saluation ; but

we

(e) Sunday no Sabbath. pag. 12.

(f) Ibid. pag. 10.

wee neither doe, nor can yeelde,
that *Proteſtancie* is compatible with
eternall happineſſe. For, to allow
ſaluation for men, diſagreeing in
Faith, Religion, and Communion, is one of the greateſt abſurdi-
ties in *Turciſme*, or *Socinianiſme* ;
and is but diſguiſed *Atheiſme*. Wee
then are ſafe by your owne confeſ-
ſion; but you cannot bee ſo, without repentance, and reunion to our
Church. Beſides, if our Church en-
ioyed all things neceſſary to Saluation : how can *Proteſtants* bee excuſed
from the grieuous ſinne of formall
Schiſme, who ſeparated from that
Church, for points confeſſedly not ne-
neceſſary to ſaluation? Yea, how are
they not guilty of *Schiſme*, who for-
ſooke that Church, which, before *Luther*, was only true Church, if our Sauiour Chriſt had any viſible Church
vpon earth? And what heighth of dangerous madnes is it, to leaue a Church,
which cannot erre in points neceſſarie
to Saluation; and ioyne in *beliefe* and
Communion, with priuate perſons, who
may deceaue, and be deceaued, euen in
fundi-

fundamentall articles of Faith? And I would gladly know, with what visible Church exiſting before *Luther*, did hee ioyne, when vpon pretence of Reformation, hee departed from all Churches extant, when hee firſt appeared; and conſequently how can hee auoide the iuſt imputation of *Schiſme*? But I will not vrge theſe points here, referring my ſelfe, to what hath beene ſaid in *Charitie maintained* and euen to what will appeare in thoſe very *Motiues*, which induced the *Anſwerer* himſelfe to leaue *Proteſtatiſme*; and afterward being reſolued, not to remaine Catholicke, as not conducing to his temporall ends, hee finally plunged himſelfe in *Sociniaiſme*, ſeeing full well, that his owne *Motiues* could not bee anſwered in the grounds of *Proteſtants*. But it is time to returne, and ſhew, that I ſpoke not without ground, in accuſing *Socinians* in generall, of ſuch vnchriſtian doctrines, as you haue heard, ſince you will ſee my word made good in *particular* Tenets of one of them, which at this

fit

28

fit occasion came to my hands; and I willingly impart them to the Reader, as they were giuen me; yet so, as in charitie I conceale the partie taxed with them, no otherwise then I forbeare to publish the name of the *Answearer*. If guiltinesse driue any one to aske : (*g*) *Nunquid ego sum, Rabbi? Maister*, am I he? And that hee chance to be answered (*h*) : *Tu dixisti*; Thou hast said so; the blame and shame must rest on himselfe alone, who alone would be discouering himselfe.

(*g*)*Matb. c. 26. v. 25.*
(*h*)*Ibid.*

CHAP. III.

Diuerse enormous Heresies, maintained by a certaine Socinian, *contrary either to the* 39. *Articles of the Church of* England, *or to the Faith of all* Christians.

1. THat the Sonne of God is not begotten, from euerlasting, of the Father : is not very, and eternall God, of one substance with the Father; and that two whole and

and perfect natures were not ioyned in one perſon. *Cont. Art.* 2.

2. That Chriſt did not aſcend into Heauen, in his Bodie, with Fleſh, Bones, and all things appertaining to the perfection of mans nature. *Cont. Art.* 4.

3. That the Holy Ghoſt doth not proceede from the Father, and the Sonne; nor is of one ſubſtance with the Father, and the Sonne, true and eternall God. *Cont. Art.* 5.

4. That all the Books of the Old and New Teſtament, as they are commonly receaued, are not equall in the authoritie, and infallibility of holy Scripture. *Cont. Art.* 6.

5. That the three Creeds ought not throughly to bee receaued, and belieued; for that they may be diſproued by moſt certaine warrants of holy Scripture; and that among other falſhoods in the Creed of *Saint Athanaſius*, this is one, that if a man disbelieue any part of that Creed, without doubt, hee ſhall periſh euerlaſtingly: That the Apoſtles Creed, is no certaine and authenticall Tradition; and

that

that the Article of *Holy Catholicke Church*, is not necessarily to be belieued. *Cont. Art.* 8.

6. That Originall sinne is not the fault and corruption of the nature of euery man; nor deserues Gods wrath and damnation. *Cont. Art.* 9.

7. That any man may bee saued by the Law or Sects which hee professeth; so that hee bee diligent to frame his life according to that Law, and the light of Nature. *Cont. Art.* 18.

8. That the Church hath no authority in Controuersies of Faith, to oblige any mans conscience. *Cont. Art.* 20.

9. That the Sacraments bee only Badges, or Tokens of Christian mens profession. *Cont. Art.* 25. 27. And that they bee not necessary to saluation. *Cont. Catechism. Protestant. Anglic.*

10. That the Baptisme of young Children is not to bee retained in the Church, as most agreable to the institution of Christ. *Cont. Art.* 27.

11. That the offering of Christ vpon the Crosse, is not a perfect propitiation and satisfaction for all the sins of the whole world. *Cont. Art.* 31.

12. That the true Body and Blood of Chrift is not in the Bleffed Sacrament, neither in a *Reall* nor *Spirituall* manner; and that it is only a figne or token of his Body. *Cont. Art.* 28.

13. That Faith containes no infallible certaintie of the things belieued.

14. That the reafonable Soule is not immortall, naturall; and *per fe*, but only *per accidens*; as it is added to fome Soules, by way of punifhment or reward, to be immortall.

15. That this immortality of wicked Soules is not to bee extended, neither to all eternity; and that it were vniuft in God, to punifh finite offences, with infinite torments.

16. That no point of Chriftian Religion is to be belieued aboue Reafon.

For an *Epilogue* to thefe groffe errors, I could adde an *Apologue* of his owne, and lay in his difh a couple of *Frogs.* He vnderftands my meaning. (a)

Tell mee now, Chriftian Reader, what manner of man this *Socinian* is; and what it is to be a *Socinian*, or *Proteftant*, or any other *Sectary*, denying the infallibility of Gods Church in all her definitions, concerning matters

(a) If the Anfwerer publifh his Booke, and yet will not declare his opinion concerning euerie one of thefe wicked Pofitions: by omitting to plead not guiltie in that occafion, euery zealous Chriftian will hold him to bee guiltie of them all.

matters of Faith? For, as I haue said already, whosoeuer refuseth to relie on such Authoritie, must resolue the truth of his Faith, into the strength of his owne *wit*, or, to speake more truely, of his *will*, which is to take away all *infallible*, *supernaturall Faith*; without which (as the (*b*) Apostle auoucheth) *it is impossible to please God.*

(b) *Heb.* *c. 11. v. 6.*

And thus hauing shewed, what *Socinianisme* is, and vpon what ground it goes; I may now oportunely deliuer the *Answerer* his *direction*, least hee chance to mistake, and in lieu of maintaining *Protestancie*, hiddenly plant poison of *Socianisme*, and leaue *Charitie maintained*, not so much as once spoken to, in his whole *Answer*, as I noted in the beginning.

CHAP.

CHAP. IV.

*What the Answerer is to obserue, if
he will speake to any purpose.*

Irst it will be expected, that he
declare his owne opinion plainely
and particularly; and not thinke to satisfie by a meere destructiue (a) way of
obiecting such difficulties against Catholicks, as, vpon examination, tend
to the ouerthrow of all Religion, no
lesse then of Catholicke Doctrine.

Secondly, that his arguments destroy not some of his owne Tenets.

Thirdly, that he contradict not
D. *Potter*, whome he pretends to de-
fende; and who maintaines the infallibilitie of Gods Church, in *fundamentall* Articles; the Supernaturalitie of
Faith; and diuers other points, which
I know the *Answerer* laughes at.

Fourthly, that he oppose not the 39.
Articles of the Church of *England*.

Fiftly, that his grounds destroy not
the beliefe of the most Blessed Trinitie,

(a) Sed qua
rursum ra-
tio reuoca-
bat, ne apud
eos (Mani-
chaos) peni-
tus hærerem
nisi quod ip-
sos quoque
animaduerte-
bam, plus in
refellendis
aliis diser-
tos, & copio-
sos esse,
quàm in suis
probandis
firmos &
certos ma-
neres S. Aug.
De vtilitat.
Creden.
cap. 1.

G   the

the Deitie of our deare Lord and Sauiour, and of the Holy Ghost; Originall sinne, and diuers other doctrines,
which all good Christians belieue; yea
and all verities, that cannot be proued
by naturall Reason.

Sxithly, that he relie not vpon such
Principles, as must bring with them
the deniall of diuers Bookes of holy
Scripture, receaued into the *Canon*,
both by Catholicks and Protestants.
And if he asked, whether the Epistle
of *Saint Iames*, the Apocalyps of *Saint
Iohn*, with some other parts of Scripture, now receaued by English Protestants, though heretofore controuer-
ted, be Canonicall, let him not still
thinke, to satisfie, by saying : *These
are captious questions.*

Seauenthly, that he doe not ouerthrow the infallibility of all Scripture, both of the Old and New Testament.

Eighthly, that his Arguments tend
not to proue an impossibilitie of all
Diuine *Supernaturall infallible Faith*
and Religion, that either hath been,
or is, or shall be, or possibly can be.

But

But now, the reason, why I preuent the *Answerer*, with these *Directions*, is this, From Truth, no man can, by good consequence, inferre falshood. If then the *Answerer* produce such Arguments, as either proue nothing, or els must extend to proue that, which is confessedly false, it will remaine very cleare, that his reasons are but Sophismes, and artificiall falsities, though they should seeme not easie to be answered, especially to such, as are either not learned at all, or superficially learned, and not versed in solid *Philosophie*, or *Schoole Diuinitie*, from whence *Socinians* are glad to borrow *Obiections*, but either dissemble, or vnderstand not the *Solutions*. Wherefore, if the Arguments of the *Answerer* be found to beate vpon some of the foresayd grounds, and by that meanes appeare to proue *too much*, euerie one will see, they proue *nothing at all*. And if (notwithstanding this *Direction* to the contrarie) he will be trenching on the sayd excesses, his Booke is already answered, euen before it appeare.

C2   But

But let him not interpret this my preuention, or Direćton, to proceede from feare, that his Booke will be vnanfwerable, and that therefore I feeke afore hand to difgrace the Authour, and foreftall the publication: For by Gods holie afsiftance, his Booke fhall be anfwered, and the latent venome fetcht out, though perhaps he will *lay wagers to the contrarie*: and with his much confidence would perfwade *All Soules* to belicue him. And in truth, what greater aduantage could wee wifh againft Proteftants, then that they fhould truft their Caufe, and pofsibilitie to by faued, with a Champion, who often and euen not very long fince, hath profeffed, that he will neuer fubfcribe to their 39. *Articles*? and hath fet downe in writing, *Motiues*, which induced him to forfake *Proteftantifme* (to which indeed he neuer returned) and which are extant ftill to be exhibited, if need be, vnder his owne hand. But howfoeuer, I prefente a copie of them, in the next, which fhall be the laft, Chapter of my *Direćtion*.

CHAP.

CHAP. V.

The Motiues, *for which the Answerer forsooke* Protestantisme.

1. BEcause perpetuall visible profession, which could neuer be wanting to the Religion of Christ, nor any part of it, is apparently wanting to Protestant Religion; so farre as concernes the points in contestation.

2. Because *Luther* and his followers, separating from the Church of *Rome,* separated also from all Churches, pure or impure, true or false then being in the world; vpon which ground I conclude, that either Gods promises did faile of performance, if there were then no Church in the world, which held all things necessarie, and nothing repugnant to Saluation; or els that *Luther* and his Sectaries, separating from all Churches then in the world, and so from the

C 3　true,

true, if there were any true, were
damnable Schismaticks.

3. Because, if any credit may be giuen
to as creditable records, as any are extant, the doctrine of Catholicks hath
beene frequently confirmed ; and the
opposite doctrine of Protestants, confounded, with supernaturall and diuine Miracles.

4. Because many points of Protestant doctrine, are the damned opinions
of Hereticks, condemned by the Pri-
mitiue Church.

5. Because the Prophecies of the old
Testament, touching the Conuersion of
Kings & Nations to the true Religiō of
Christ, haue been accomplished in & by
the Catholicke *Roman* Religion, & the
Professors of it ; and not by Protestant
Religion, and the Professors of it.

6. Because the doctrine of the
Church of *Rome* is conformable, and
the doctrine of Protestants contrary, to
the doctrine of the Fathers of the Pri-
mitiue Church, euen by the confession
of Protestants themselues ; I meane,
those Fathers, who liued within the
compasse of the first 600. yeares ; to
whom

whom Proteſtanrs themſelues doe very frequently,&very confidently appeale.

7. Becauſe the firſt pretended Reformers had neither extraordinary *Commiſſion* from God, nor ordinary *Miſſion* from the Church, to preach Proteſtant doctrine.

8. Becauſe *Luther*, to preach againſt the Maſſe (which containes the moſt materiall points now in Controuerſie) was perſwaded by reaſons ſuggeſted to him by the Diuell himſelfe, diſputing with him. So himſelfe profeſſeth in his Booke *de Miſſa Priuata*. That all men might take heed of following him, who profeſſeth himſelf to follow the diuell.

9. Becauſe the Proteſtant Cauſe is now, & hath been from the beginning, maintained with groſſe falſifications, and Calumnies; whereof their prime Controuerſie writers, are notoriouſly, and in high degree guiltie.

10. Becauſe by denying all humane authority, either of Pope, or Councels, or Church, to determine Controuerſies of Faith, they haue aboliſhed all poſſible meanes of ſuppreſsing Hereſie, or reſtoring vnity to the Church.

C 4　　　　Theſe

These were the *Answerers Motiues*; and they are good ones indeed, and so strong, that he could neuer since frame his minde to *Protestancie* : And the Profession of Catholicke Religion, not suting with his desires & designes, as I said before, he fell vpon *Socinianisme*, that is, a *No Religion*. I will not here ponder the foresaid *Motiues* only I must say, as I noted in the precedent Chapter, that since they all (except perchance the last) chiefly concerne matter of *Fact*, rather then any subtile points of *Doctrine*, he cannot with any probable shew of reason, retract them, and if he should, yet who would not sooner credit his sinceritie, whilst he speakes, against the current of the times, in this place, and contrarie to worldlie hopes, then now, when all human respects concurre to sway his words, profession, and carriage, when contrary to his inward thoughts? But in the meane time, it would be sport, to behold *Doctor Potter* confuting these *Motiues* of the *Answerer*, while he is pretending to defend *Doctor Potter*. And it may well seeme a
strange

ſtrange and prepoſterous zeale in the *Anſwerer* (if he haue any regard to the Church of *England*) to haue been ſo long careleſſe in remouing this ſcandall againſt *Proteſtants,* and anſwering his owne *Motiues*; and yet now to ſhew ſuch feruour in writing againſt others: which whether he doe of his owne accord, or by entreatie of *Doctor Potter*, or from ſome *Higher command*, I am neither certaine, nor ſollicitous. My hartie wiſhes are, that whoſoeuer ſhall reade theſe *Motiues*, may, for the eternall good of his owne Soule, conſider them with indifferencie, and at leaſure, and neuer reſt from ſolliciting the learnedſt *Proteſtants*, either to giue him ſatisfaction (which is impoſsible to be donne.) or els not take it ill, if he haſten to the One, alwaies Viſible, Catholicke, Apoſtolicke, Roman Church; out of which none can, without preſumption, hope to be ſaued, and of which Bleſſed * *Saint Auſtin* ſaith: *Numerate Sacerdotes vel ab ipſa Petri ſede; & in ordine illo Patrum, quis cui ſucceſſit, videte. Ipſa eſt Petra; quam non vincunt*

* *Cont. part. Donati Pſal.*

vincunt superba inferorum portæ; Rec-
kon the Priests, euen from the very Sea
of *Peter*; and see, who succeeded
one another in that ranke of Fathers. That is the Rocke, againſt
which the proud gates
of Hell doe not
preuaile.
(∵)

F I N I S.